Singing

to the

North Wind

The Calling to an Extraordinary Life

Advance Praise for
Singing to the North Wind...

"Susannah conjures a wild and sacred landscape, writing with a strong voice and clear heart of her spirit-led life. This book will be an inspiration and a comfort to many who are seeking validation and understanding regarding their own spirit-led life adventures."

~ Nicholas Breeze Wood,
shamanic practitioner,
publisher of *Sacred Hoop Magazine*

"Singing to the North Wind is a brave book. Susannah invites the reader into the experience of learning to trust her own callings, gifts, skill, intuition, and wisdom to create a life that is uniquely and richly her own. Susannah reminds us that each life has its shape and that our job is to listen to the wisdom of our own hearts and to follow that guidance wherever it leads us, regardless of the perceptions of others, and the strange and difficult challenges that may arise. In doing so we create self-trust and deep alliances with others that support the expression of our truest nature."

~ Temple Crocker,
interdisciplinary artist and somatic educator

"A deep, intimate, and powerful view of a life lived well in service to the Gods, Ancestors, and spirits. Rising from a world which has not understood them, and through hard work, discipline, and initiation, becoming a jeweler, sacred smith, and shaman, Susannah Ravenswing invites you to experience their story."

~ Sarenth Odinsson,
Heathen spiritworker

"This extraordinary book is a significant achievement. As an academic, I never fully understood what 'oral history' meant, but now it is very clear. You have been able to translate and transcribe a collection of experiences that most people would have difficulty understanding, with raw eloquence."

~ David Franklyn Williams,
Professor, Winston-Salem, North Carolina
and Cape Town, South Africa;
Fellow of the Learned Society of Wales

Singing
to the
North Wind
The Calling to an Extraordinary Life

Susannah Ravenswing

VANADIS PUBLISHING

First edition 2022

ISBN: 979-8-9868310-0-8 (paperback)
ISBN: 979-8-9868310-1-5 (hardcover)
ISBN: 979-8-9868310-2-2 (ebook)

Forward by Liam. M. Hooper
Cover design by Diana C. Coe
Cover photo by Stephanie Berbek
Author photo by Eric M. Livengood
Dancing Fog B&W courtesy Joseph - stock.adobe.com
Cherry Blossom Branch courtesy asemeykin - stock.adobe.com
Am Bienenstock (Bee) courtesy C. Schüßler - stock. adobe.com
Great Horned Owl courtesy natureguy - stock.adobe.com

Excerpts from *The Duergarbok: The Dwarves of the Northern Tradition* by Susannah Ravenswing (Asphodel Press, 2019).
Reprinted with permission.

For Ken Bradstock:

Teacher, Healer, Writer, Mentor, and Cherished Friend.

You listened and believed.

Table of Contents

NOTE: The events described in this book are a true accounting of my own personal experience. Individuals mentioned will have their own perspectives, which are unique to them and may differ from my own. This is the nature of reality, that we each experience it through the lens of our being. There is no single true reality, only a collection of subjective ones.

Foreword
by Liam M. Hooper

On a warming day in the late winter of 2016, I made my first visit to TwoTrees—the charmed, forest-nestled otherworld that is slightly hidden in the foothills and is home to Susannah Ravenswing. I had become generally acquainted with Susannah through shared connections in our local Pagan and Heathen communities. Outside of these larger group gatherings, however, we had not had occasion to spend significant time together. Yet, I had already sensed that Susannah was a trustworthy and interesting person. Since I believe serendipitous, beneficent moments, when present, should be heeded, I accepted the offer to visit with Susannah when it was extended.

Around a table lit by south-facing windows and replete with various spiritual tools, amid songs lifted to gods and ancestors, the spirit was present and moving—as tangible as the sunlight. In those spirit-filled moments of our first visit, I understood I was in the presence of someone rare, indeed—a truly kind, genuine person, void of ulterior agendas and shallow transactionalism, invested in striving for meaningful, authentic living, as well as friendships built on communal ground, care, honesty, and reciprocity.

The frankness and openness with which Susannah weaves her story in *Singing to the North Wind*, too, reveals these valued qualities. Through poetry, portions of journal entries, and storytelling, Susannah takes us, as readers, through her life and her shamanic awakening. Structured amidst poetry, beginning in the winter and moving through the fall of an allegorical year, we journey with Susannah through the formative movements of her life experiences, lessons, sorrows, triumphs, trials, and transformations.

To be sure, as her call is to an extraordinary life, this is no ordinary, run-of-the-presses memoir. Among the pages, in typeset words and the white spaces between, in visions shared and daily life related, the spirits are astir. Susannah reveals other worlds to us, introduces us to other realities around us, and invites us to look and listen, fearlessly, with her. Along the way, perhaps, if we dare, we might find glimpses of our own lives, our own half-forgotten experiences, our own dream-world realities gazing back at us, showing us familiar faces.

In the midst of this unique encounter, a larger story of shamanism appears to us. For those who may not be familiar with this kind of spiritual practitioner, a shaman journeys within and between many worlds, engages multiple realities (often simultaneously), and interacts relationally with the inhabitants of all these interconnected, vibrant, and vital worlds. Shamans do these things in service to the beings, human and not-so-human, Gods, spirits, and ancestors who walk with them. It is, as Susannah's story reveals, not an easy path, nor is it conventional in our contemporary culture. Yet, she reminds us that shamans have always been with us, even when misunderstanding and fear made it dangerous for them to make themselves known openly.

The shamanic life intersects with other lifeways that, across time and cultures, have been vilified and, often, erased. As we read along on Susannah's journey, we discover with her that throughout history shamans were often gender-transcendent persons — people who, in our modern context, we might understand as transgender, non-binary, agender, gender non-conforming, and/or intersex. With trust and authenticity, Susannah also openly and frankly shares this aspect of her shamanic life with us, as well as her discovery of the correlations between gender-transcendence and a lived, practical mysticism. In marvelous and mystery-revealing ways, Susannah's story lays bare before us the many layers, seen and unseen, through which the relational cosmos intersects and interacts with our lives, as well as the many ways in which we may come to be aware of, enchanted by, and shaped and formed by, the living forces and beings around us.

To make this point, I want to argue, briefly, that relationship is the core nature and functional necessity of everything in the universe — and that the essence of our humanity is to be in relationship with one another. In fact, physics assures us the essence of everything from atomic particles to trees, streams, and human beings is relationality. Moreover, our relational connections are not only the path to fuller understanding of ourselves and our world, but these relational interactions are also the way we change the world because they, first, change us. Our relationships with others expand us, teach us, help shape and form us, even as we — whether we realize it or not — help shape and form our world, personally and collectively. This is the way we are made. This is the way of things in this vast, diversity-drenched, mystery-laden, magical cosmos we inhabit.

In these pages, Susannah does indeed reveal the ways that

such easily overlooked realities are right here in our midst if only we open ourselves to them. In the hands of such a skilled shaman, we might even come to an understanding of those palpable, frustratingly intangible but no less transformative moments in our lives that we pushed into the recesses of our memories where we store the things we cannot yet apprehend. At the very least, this book speaks forth its subjects in a voice reminiscent of ancient, bardic poetry and by offering forgotten pieces of history, teachings, and other insights gained only through the telling (and receiving) of a good story.

In short, we live in a world woefully devoid of mystery, dismissive of anything that cannot be objectively seen, touched, acquired, or consumed — a world generally distrusting of people who reveal to us the presence of other realities. In fact, we live in a season when the relationship between humanity and the natural world is particularly fraught, placing our future, perhaps even our very survival at risk.

Into this world Susannah dares to speak, inviting us to walk with her, tarry a while, and encounter not only the place of TwoTrees and the extraordinary path of her life but also the fullness of our own humanity as we sit a spell, listen to her sing, and discover mysteries we have been conditioned to ignore. The Old Ways of living in collaboration with the natural world that Susannah describes provide a remarkable corrective for such a time as this. To read and encounter Susannah's life is to be compelled to expand our awareness, soften our gaze, and look at her life, the world around us, and our own experiences, not through the eyes of Western society and modern civilization, but through our own inner eyes — the eyes the world has taught us to keep closed.

Doubtless, some of Susannah's experiences are far from common. This is as it should be, as this, too, is how we are made — personally particular, individually unique, yet humanly and relationally similar enough to encounter one another and to be changed for the better. Thus, in receiving Susannah's story, I invite you not only to receive knowledge, poetry, and good storytelling bardic prose but also to meet my soul-friend and my spirit-sibling. I have no doubt that those who choose to walk with Susannah will find themselves changed by the journey with this powerful teacher, much as I have.

Liam Hooper
Author, *Trans-Forming Proclamation*
Winston Salem, NC
September 2021

Introduction

I am a short, heavy, masculine-looking 69-year-old Caucasian woman, happily married and the mother of adult twin sons.

I am a Seer, a Healer, a sacred Maker, a Lore-Keeper, and a Teacher.

I am a Skald, a Seidhkona, a Spaekona, and a Gythja in the Northern Tradition.

I am a Shaman, a calling that dates back to Paleolithic times, and, as such, I walk two worlds: that of ordinary consensual reality and another, the sacred realms of Gods and spirits, serving as a bridge between the Holy Powers and my clients.

I heal people; I heal the land.

I have lived an extraordinary life, and this is my story.

Season One

Winter, Dreamtime

Hunger stalks the iron-hard earth
And an old stag falls.
Arctic air swirls the scent of snow,
Light to counter darkness, muffle sound,
Revealing mouse paths
And the impressions where the deer lie,
Their grayed coats like laden skies,
Breath offered to the stillness.
This is a cruel time, filled with challenges,
A time to conserve, to endure, to dream.
While frozen branches crack and groan,
Thrashed by storm winds
And bowed beneath their icy burden,
All life drops toward stillness, rests,
Then leans toward spring.
The storm sweeps northward and
As the clouds break,
Moonlight silvers newly-fallen snow—
A promissory note of light to come.

One
REMEMBERING

Pale light filters through the gaps between the hides draped over arching mastodon tusks, and smoke rises from the firepit to slip through the central opening. An old man bows over a soapstone bowl, singing softly. His silver hair trails across wiry bronze shoulders, and he wears a ceremonial headpiece made from the body of an eagle, the beak falling forward over his forehead. Outside, his community gathers silently, respectful of the risk he will undertake on their behalf. Their supply of dried meat grows low, and the hunters have been unsuccessful in their search for game. Soon, the snows will come. A bladder filled with water has been hung over the fire. When it begins to boil, the old woman who is both wife and assistant tips a portion carefully into the stone bowl and backs out of the tent. He must journey alone.

Cradling the warming bowl in his gnarled hands, he sings a blessing to the spirit of water. Tiny bubbles rise to greet him. With a prayer, he opens a pouch by his knee and takes out the dried caps of mushrooms, the ones the reindeer love to eat, lifting them high as he sings to greet them. Crumbling them into the hot water, he picks up a rattle made of reindeer dewclaws strung on a loop of hide and finds the rhythmic clicking sound of hundreds of migrating hooves. The liquid in the bowl darkens, absorbing his prayers, and when the moment is right, he drinks the contents, chewing the bitter rehydrated fungi. Laying the bowl aside, he resumes his rattling and adds a song to call his most powerful ally, the Golden Eagle.

His eyes water and fall closed. Chills wrack him, and he retches. He rocks, feeling the ache that accompanies the shift in his energy body, long arm bones stretching to form mighty wings. Then, with a powerful thrust, he sends his consciousness forth, up through the smoke hole, soaring across the vast expanse of gray-green tundra. Borne upward on the north wind, he scouts for the migrating herd, finding them far to the south on their way to a river crossing below dark cliffs where the flow is shallow and broad. His task accomplished, he draws his consciousness back into his man's body, gradually becoming aware of the dying fire before him. He sings a prayer of thanksgiving and uses his flint knife to slash his palm, offering lifeblood for life.

On unsteady legs, he rises and emerges from the tent to be greeted by the clan's primary hunters. "They are coming," he announces. "You must leave tonight if you are to be there when they cross at the shallows at the black rocks." He gazes at the women, gathered with their children further back. "And you — remember to keep the taboos if you want your men to bring home meat and hides! Put away your needles and sleep alone!"

His wife rises and comes forward so that he can lean on her, leading him back into the tent to their bed, padded with furs. There she feeds him soup made with bitter herbs to help counteract the toxins in the mushrooms, berries she picked and dried the previous summer, and a knob of precious rich fat to replace the energy he has expended on the clan's behalf. He nods, then sleeps, his job done. His clan will not starve.

Two
THE OLD ROAD

Witch Doctor. Medicine Man. Root Worker. Pejorative terms used by white folks long disconnected from their native spiritual and healing heritages with the assumption of a social superiority attained through science and a rigid interpretation of reality. In many cultures, stories surviving from pre-Colonial times describe the roles of Indigenous healers and wise individuals serving their people as an interface with the natural and spiritual worlds. We have evidence that such specialist practitioners have existed since Paleolithic times in their images on cave walls and in bones, stones, and antlers carved with sacred symbols. Among "Two Leggeds" there have always been those who were different, who saw and experienced the world(s) in alternate ways. Such differences can be useful. They can also get one labeled "crazy" or even killed. I am one of "those people." I am a Shaman, trained, initiated, and proclaimed as such by my community.

The word "shaman" derives from the Siberian Tungusic Evenki word *šamán*, meaning "frenzy," and refers to a spiritual practitioner who serves their community through counsel, intercession, and healing accomplished through consultation with, and assistance from, helping Spirits accessed by entering altered states of consciousness. Such a practice presumes an animist worldview: that all things are inspirited Beings rather than inanimate objects and thus are worthy of respect, that they, as Beings, have agency and thus must be negotiated with. It is a belief system grounded in reciprocity, give and take, collaboration and cooperation.

Shamanistic practices exist in Indigenous cultures the world over, surviving despite the concerted efforts of religions and government systems to stamp them out. The Catholic Church burned village healers at the stake, calling them "Witches." The Lutheran Church did the same to the Sámi Noaidi. The Communist regimes of the Soviet Union and China brutally persecuted the traditional shamans of Siberia and Mongolia. Even today, in Africa and Brazil, traditional healers are murdered by self-righteous evangelical Christians who consider their work "of the Devil."

The term "shamanism" is perhaps best known for its use by practitioners of Core Shamanism, an amalgam originated by an American anthropologist and educator, which focuses on the empowerment of the individual and is not grounded in any particular spiritual or cultural context. To quote the official website of the Foundation for Shamanic Studies, "Core Shamanism consists of the universal, near-universal, and common features of shamanism, together with journeys to other worlds, a distinguishing feature of shamanism. As originated, researched, and developed by Michael Harner, the principles of Core Shamanism are not bound to any specific cultural group or perspective. Since the West overwhelmingly lost its shamanic knowledge centuries ago due to religious oppression, the Foundation's programs in Core Shamanism are particularly intended for Westerners to reacquire access to their rightful spiritual heritage through quality workshops and training courses."

During his studies of tribal peoples in the Amazon, Harner explored Indigenous uses of the hallucinogenic vine ayahuasca and other psychedelics, returning to the United States where he experimented with rhythmic drumming as a means of accessing similar altered states of consciousness. By the early 1970s, believing that anyone could experience significant personal revelations via the use of certain techniques, he began teaching workshops. This led to the publication of his book *The Way of the Shaman: A Guide to Power and Healing* (1980) and the establishment of the Foundation for Shamanic Studies, an income-generating pyramid of classes, workshops, and practitioner certifications. Key to Harner's "tool-kit" approach was the concept that techniques could be universalized — removed and practiced outside the cultural and spiritual context in which they developed. Core Shamanism also emphasizes positive interpretation and discounts fear, trial, and potential harm. While many practitioners find this form of practice personally meaningful and a useful process for assisting clients, it has, for others, become a revenue stream with no spiritual heart.

An alternate collection of practices, Neoshamanism has no central spiritual belief system and mixes elements drawn from various cultures and traditions as well as additional improvised elements. Practices include accessing altered states of consciousness through the ingestion of entheogens, and a lively, if clandestine, industry exists offering seekers the opportunity to experience traditional medicine plants for novelty as well as healing. More New Age in flavor, Neoshamanism de-emphasizes the existence of evil and negativity while discouraging fear — an approach that can become a form of toxic positivity. That, in some ways, makes Neoshamanism more dangerous. In contrast, traditional shamanism recognizes that these concepts fulfill constructive and essential roles in the cultural dynamic by helping to maintain social order.

Indigenous and specialist shamanic traditions, such as the Northern Traditions which I practice, tend to be initiatory and life-transforming, often calling a potential practitioner into service through life-threatening physical and psychiatric illnesses — colloquially and collectively referred to as "shaman sickness." In cultures practicing traditional shamanism, it is understood that certain individuals possess qualities that make them useful to the Gods and spirits, and thus to their community. These individuals, who are regarded as being called by the spirits or by their Ancestors, often undergo great trials and prolonged trauma and illness before accepting their calling. Such a role also involves training through apprentice-ship to an experienced shaman or spirit-training until capable of passing tests in an initiatory ceremony. The candidate's subjective experience of death, dismemberment, and rebirth culminates in a service profession rooted in a particular cul-ture's spiritual beliefs. The professional credibility of these practitioners rests wholly on their ability to serve their com-munity competently rather than on a series of certificates or external credentials.

Highly trained traditional practitioners cultivate collabo-rative relationships with helping spirits referred to as allies. A traditional shaman calls upon those allies to gather knowledge or accomplish tasks impossible to achieve in an ordinary state of consciousness (such as the example in the previous chap-ter). Most importantly, their practices are based in a particular and specific spiritual context and belief system, which does not seek to be universal (as in Core Shamanism or Neosha-manism), but is informed by place and culture.

Thus, my practice as a traditional shaman is tied not just to the land in general, but to specific places. For me, most sig-nificant is the relationship I have developed with TwoTrees, the tract of land where I reside. At the same time, I am deeply connected with Scotland, Scandinavia, and the steppe lands of Central Asia. I refer to this relationship with both the land and the Holy Powers as "votive," a term sharing Latin roots with "devout," as it couples shamanic practice with a religious or spiritual framework. Indigenous cultures—those not damaged by colonialism—are inherently animist. By this, I mean that their worldview and beliefs have been profoundly shaped by the natural environment in which they reside. They exist in relationship to the land, knowing that their wellness, perhaps even their survival, is dependent upon right relationship with All Beings. It is the reverence for reciprocal relationship that the modern world has lost and so desperately needs to relearn.

These spiritual traditions, rooted in the hunter-gatherer cultures of the Paleolithic era, emphasize a collaborative relationship with the natural world, respect for one's Gods and Ancestors, and the cultivation of personal wholeness. A core task of the traditional shaman is to negotiate and maintain balance among the Gods, spirits (both helpful and harmful), Ancestors, natural forces, and the community of humans that the shaman serves. Many of the challenges of the human condition are seen to be resulting from imbalances in these relationships. "Balance" is a concept common to many traditional healing systems and is increasingly significant in Western holistic healing. It is no coincidence that the words "heal" and "whole" share a common origin in the proto-Germanic word "*hailaz*," or that the concept of wholeness contains within it the idea that the component parts are in balance. A whole and balanced person is a well person, a person who thrives in their life.

In the Eurasian cultures in which the term "shaman sickness" originated, it was collectively understood and accepted that particular individuals might be called by the Gods and their Ancestors to serve as shamans, that the burden of such a life might be onerous, and thus resisted. Resisting such a calling might result in a variety of grave and even life-threatening illnesses. At the same time, for persons in the West, the term "shaman sickness," commonly encountered on the Internet, is problematic, in that it invites individuals who are experiencing bewildering and overwhelming life experiences and circumstances to conclude that their misfortunes are indicators that they are somehow called to the sacred and deeply challenging life of a shaman.

It might be noted here that the line between madman and mystic is a fine one. The famed 12th-century Christian abbess Hildegard of Bingen wrote of experiencing God through all five senses, suggesting that she experienced Synesthesia, a neurological condition in which the senses are cross-wired, with numbers, colors, and musical pitches often interrelated. Experiencing deep trances and vivid spiritual visions from childhood, Hildegard became gravely ill after deciding to cease speaking or writing about her visions. Only when she again began to share her revelations did her health return. This pattern bears remarkable similarity to "shaman sickness."

To walk a path of service, for that most surely is what a shaman is called to, one must become comfortable with the concept of revelation and personal gnosis — information and guidance that reveals itself within the individual practitioner. Many spiritual paths find their basis in a body of lore and historical practices. Some are openly reconstructionist.

Our shamanic lineages were destroyed by the church throughout Europe and in many parts of the world, and our shamanic practices were obliterated or demonized. The limited historical references we have are filtered through the spiritual and cultural agendas of forced conversion. This lack of intact traditions has forced practitioners of the Northern Traditions to become spiritual archaeologists. The careful observation of related and intact cultures offers additional insights and wisdom. However, ultimately, shamans of the Northern Traditions must learn to be open to internal revelations upon which one is compelled to act, regardless of any external confirmation or precedent or lack thereof. This requires one to learn to distinguish the everyday internal conversations (such as, "Remember to wash the sheets and take the roast out to thaw") from the voices of the Gods and spirits directing one to do something: *Go into the forest and build a fire, and I will come to you.*

As human beings, we grow up in a society that teaches through affirmation or the lack thereof. When we do as our parents, teachers, or general society demand and fulfill their expectations, we are rewarded with acceptance (more or less). When we either cannot conform or refuse to do so, we are at risk of shaming, ostracization, or even harm. To hear one's own inner voice making commentary or reminding one of some task or responsibility is considered "normal" and thus socially acceptable. To hear voices from "others" is deemed to be odd at best—and a sign of mental illness at worst. There-fore, we are socialized from an early age to disregard the spirit voices that might otherwise instruct, inform, and enliven us. As a result, we who are born with such inner guidance often resist service to forces greater than ourselves until we no lon-ger can, and the pain arising from the denial of our authentic self demands that we must come to terms with lived reality. And, then, we begin the long process of accepting ourselves as we are. By accepting who we are, we have the opportunity to open more deeply in alignment with the will of the Holy Powers

We have been taught to refer to consensual reality as "The World." However, animistic traditions often acknowledge lay-ers of reality, which they refer to as "worlds" (plural). To serve as a shaman is a way of being in relationship with and expe-riencing these worlds, of nurturing tradition and stretching ourselves to understand as our Ancestors did. Unfortunately, opportunities for competent training and guidance are scarce, so we must find our way through the wilderness, learning as we go.

When folks learn that I am a shaman, they often respond,

"Oh wow! I've always thought that must be really cool." My response is that no one in their right mind would choose this path if they knew the trials and sacrifices it entails.

I have been asked why I choose to use the term shaman rather than referring to myself as a *Völva*, *Seidhkona*, or *Spaekona*, culturally specific terms for Norse female spiritual practitioners. While those terms might be applicable, they are likely to be unfamiliar to the great majority of clients who seek me out and who are far more likely to have at least some frame of reference for what a shaman might do. I also refer to myself as a spirit worker, since I quite literally work with spirits. Most importantly, I am guided by the instruction of my patron deity, Freyja.

Mine is a life of service, a life shaped by trauma and by beauty, by ignorance and by wonder. I follow the shamanic traditions and practices of my Ancestors — herders and wanderers who made their way from the vast emptiness of northern Eurasia, through taiga and tundra, across the seas of grass to the lands of the Norse. I undertake my work in service to my clients and my spirits. I follow it because my life shaped me to do so and because the Goddess I serve called me back from the brink of death and remade me in Her service.

Three
RAW MATERIAL

Among my Celtic, Scandinavian, Germanic, and Sámi ancestors were individuals with what my mother called "The Gift." They were present in my father's line, too. This Gift was expressed in a variety of ways: premonitions that showed events yet to happen or alerted for danger, hearing or knowing the thoughts or emotions of a loved one far away, and occasionally mediumship, the ability to communicate with the Dead. The Gift was strong in my mother and her mother, a Virginia mountain granny who read the future in tea leaves and playing cards for those who sought her out. It was also strong in my paternal grandmother, a well-educated and dignified woman who only acknowledged her precognitive dreams and visions in the privacy of her journal. The Gift makes one useful. It also makes one feared as different and subject to persecution.

Certain personal anomalies seem to offer fertile ground for this sacred calling. Among tribal people, many eventually called as shamans begin their lives struggling with autism, schizophrenia and other conditions that mark them as outsiders; conditions which, remarkably, often resolve or become less problematic once they begin their shamanic studies. Unlike practitioners of Core Shamanism, many of my colleagues working with the Northern Traditions are neurodivergent, atypically gendered, and struggle with obscure and often painful medical issues. In addition to diagnoses such as intersex and autistic, these medical issues include autoimmune disorders, endocrine and connective tissue disorders, and terrible migraines.

I have Congenital Adrenal Hyperplasia (CAH), an obscure

endocrine condition that caused me to be born intersex. I had genitalia that were a combination of male and female. In 1952, the medical standard for addressing my intersex variation was surgery. So, as an infant, my male parts were altered or removed, my urethra was re-routed, and I was surgically, legally, and socially assigned a female gender. CAH would also contribute to my short stature, robust bone structure, and my heaviness. Meanwhile, the series of surgeries to make my genitalia look "female" left painful scar tissue that impaired my ability to experience sexual pleasure.

I will never know how much my parents were told or understood about why their baby needed so many surgeries; I only know they never discussed it with me. As far as they were concerned, I was female. I was in my fifties before an old-time OB-GYN nurse dropped the bomb during an annual pelvic exam, casually explaining to the student accompanying her what had been done to "normalize" me. Both of these medical providers employed to care for me seemed oblivious to my shock and anger. These revelations confirmed what I had long suspected. Yet, it was another decade before I met someone else with my same condition.

My parents met and married in the golden days following the Second World War; he was a tax collector, a job he hated, and she was a bank teller. Their personal issues, along with the environment I grew up in, all played a profound role in shaping me. It was not just my physiological quirks and neurodivergent mind that made me a natural for my ancient profession, but it was also the circumstances of my childhood. When I was an infant, my father took a position as a park ranger, eventually working his way up to superintendent of a large state park where we lived in a dark little house with knotty pine paneling, surrounded by forest. My mother, who had been a city girl, felt profoundly isolated in her new life—a life that became even more challenging when she almost died giving birth to my younger brother, Reid.

Their marriage was not a happy one, and my mother struggled with visions, dissociation, and depression that eventually resulted in her hospitalization. I was five when she was taken away for what was then referred to as a "nervous breakdown." That summer, my brother and I stayed with my aunt and paternal grandmother, who were both educators. My time with them was profoundly formative — and I remain deeply grateful for their kindness and recognition of my intelligence, gifts and eccentricities.

My aunt and grandmother encouraged my inquisitive nature, teaching me to read and exposing me to history and the arts. Although they dutifully took us to Sunday School, our days together were filled with Shakespeare and Byron, picture books on the Italian Renaissance, and tales of the ancient Greeks, Romans, Anglo-Saxons, and Vikings. The upstairs bedroom where my brother and I stayed, with its curiously angled ceiling and old iron beds in which my father and his siblings had previously slept, held towering bookcases stuffed with yellow-bound issues of *National Geographic* dating back to the Society's founding. Each morning, awakening long before I was allowed downstairs, I explored the world through those volumes.

When my chastened mother returned home, my father engaged a woman of mixed African-American and Cherokee heritage to assist with the house and child care back at the park. Juana often took me along on her walks with her elderly mother, known as Birdie, who served the local Black community as healer and midwife well into her nineties. Baskets in hand, they gathered wild medicinal herbs and foraged berries and other edible fare, patiently answering my non-stop questions. As Juana's guest one summer Sunday, I experienced ecstatic worship in her tiny white-washed frame church that would forever make my mother's Methodist faith pale by comparison. While utterly plain, with two rows of backless benches and a simple pulpit, those white-washed walls bulged with Spirit I could see and feel.

The park that was my childhood home encompassed an area of the North Carolina Piedmont notable for its geology and its history. For thousands of years, the steep, eroded cores of ancient volcanoes had offered ancient people a source of rhyolite, a bluish-gray mineral ideal for the manufacture of stone tools. As such, the Uwharrie Mountains became the nexus of a native industry that entailed the quarrying and rough shaping of stone blanks and implements traded as far west as the Mississippi. In some areas of the park, the chips and flakes that were the byproducts of this industry lay several feet thick. Pottery, tools, and even burials evidenced a human residency that predated invasion by the Europeans by perhaps as much as 12,000 years.

Those Europeans found the Piedmont to be a region rich in game and other resources. Volcanic activity created veins of gold-rich quartz, which led to North Carolina's being one of the first early sources of precious metal in the United States. I was allowed to explore this remarkable environment with great freedom, and my early days in the rugged woods of the Uwharries forged in me a life-long bond with Nature.

I am lying on my side on mossy ground, looking up into a hollowed-out oak tree in our yard and conversing with the spirit of what I now know as Hericium erinaceus, or lion's mane, an important medicinal mushroom. Puzzled, my mom leans out the back door to call, "Honey, why do you have your face stuck up that tree?"

"I'm talking with Mr. Mushroom!" I turn my head to look at her, feeling the impression of stones and grass in the sweaty skin of my arms.

She makes that face, the pained one that tells me she doesn't understand. "Don't be silly. Mushrooms can't talk."

"Yes he can!" I declare adamantly.

Mom shakes her head and wipes her hands on her apron. "I don't know what to do with you," she sighs. "You just have entirely too much imagination."

My mother's reaction reflected the rationalist perspective of American culture in the 1950s and her understandable fears on my behalf. After all, her own mystic visions had been dismissed as mental illness, resulting in a deeply traumatic stint in the state psychiatric hospital where she was treated with electroconvulsive shock therapy and ice-cold showers. I was a fey and gifted child. In retrospect, I can appreciate why she might have felt it was important to suppress my strangeness. After all, to be different in the twentieth century was dangerous; it still is.

I also struggled with the sensory hypersensitivity that I now understand to be associated with being autistic. While my sensitivity is an asset in my work as a shaman, it added another bewildering layer to my childhood. Like being intersex, it was a part of me I had no words for or knowledge about. So, I couldn't factor it into my understanding of myself or how I related to the world. I just felt raw and wrong and unacceptable.

Apart from my younger brother and occasional encounters with our cousins, my early human interactions were with adults, most of whom were teachers, historians, or scientists.

They tended to be enchanted by my precociousness. By the time I started school in the fall of 1959, I read fluently but had no clue how to relate to other children.

We now realize that gender identification is a product of the brain, not the sex organs. Surgery had rearranged my body into a semblance of femaleness, but my brain told me that I was actually a boy. I felt like my body was made wrong. In the second grade, I defiantly informed my female classmates that I was a boy. This insistence resulted in my being cornered in the girls' bathroom where they forcibly removed my underpants so they could prove that I was as female as they were.

I experienced an immense amount of family pressure to be more feminine. My well-meaning mother, hoping to help me fit in, sewed pretty dresses for me and permed my dark hair. I was miserable: the lace on the dresses and billowing tulle petticoats scratched unbearably, and I felt like I was in an alien costume. Sleepovers and Barbie dolls held no interest for me—and the boys wanted nothing to do with the odd girl who wanted to talk about archaeology rather than play ball. I was an outsider: too smart, too serious, too talented in music and art. To be acceptable, to be loved, I felt compelled to embrace a persona that felt alien to me. My strangeness made me the target of intense bullying and physical violence, but no one was willing to intervene on my behalf. At the same time, I felt that my very survival, in an existential sense, was tied to being my authentic self, and, in truth, I was quite incapable of pretending to be "like other girls."

There was also that damned Gift. When my parents fought, as they did all too often, I saw the swirling dark red energy I associated with anger surrounding them, only to have them deny my perception and insist that everything was fine—even though I could clearly see otherwise. It took me a while to realize that most people didn't hear others' thoughts or sense their emotions. I clearly recall sitting in my second-grade classroom one morning and knowing one of my classmates had eaten no breakfast and was hungry, one had been beaten, and that the girl behind me was being molested by her uncle. My gift set me apart. It also made me want to be a healer, if for no other reason than to give myself a break from the pain that surrounded me! If anything, my upbringing discouraged me from holding personal boundaries, and, certainly, no one made any effort to teach me how to shield myself from the emotions of others.

"Always tell the truth!" my parents emphasized, yet when I shared what was true for me, they scolded me for making up stories. What is a child to do when their parents deny their lived reality, trying to force them to conform to an alien role in an alien world?

The intensity of my drive to be my authentic self often put me in conflict with my mother and father, who sincerely believed it was in my best interest that I comply with the expectations of Southern culture. Like many young women of that era, I was taught that I should focus on fulfilling the needs of others. As a proper Southern girl in the mid-twentieth century, I should be seen and not heard, should not challenge authority, and should not require any extra attention. In their effort to make a docile, compliant child, my parents unwittingly made me the perfect prey for predatory adults, and I experienced the first of several sexual assaults I was to experience at the hands of various family friends. My parents were too caught up in their own conflicts and issues to notice.

In retrospect, I often consider how different my life might have been had I felt supported and affirmed in my lived experience—and I am profoundly grateful to those rare individuals who offered me that gift. My peers and even my parents teased and berated me for being what they referred to as a "tomboy" — a girl who refused to be gender compliant — but no one ever suggested that I might be physiologically, energetically, or even psychologically a Being of both sexes. I was frequently scolded for being "too sensitive," as if this was some sort of character fault rather than the result of trauma or product of my inherited atypical neurology and autism. Clearly, my parents' own upbringing failed to prepare them for how to raise a child like me.

I was perhaps seven and certainly had grown beyond the necessity of a daily nap. As my mother, however, benefitted from a break from my brother and me, we were required to spend an hour or two in our rooms each afternoon. I had been given a set of different color modeling clays the previous Christmas and had figured out how to combine them to create other colors. Late in the afternoon, my mother opened my door to discover that I had turned the glass top of my dressing table into an elaborate diorama of a Native American village. Small clay figures dressed in deerskins were scraping hides, carrying in game, and smoking fish over tiny red and orange clay flames, going about daily life in rather remarkable detail.

Mom stood in the doorway, a stunned expression on her face as she murmured, "How did you do that?"

When archaeologists excavated a site located where the state was to construct the park boathouse on Lake Tillery, I begged to help sift the rusty Piedmont soil, and watched with fascination as a museum was constructed for the park visitors. For me, the process of exploring ancient history felt magical. When my third-grade teacher offered a magazine subscription to whoever finished the most books in a set period of time, I don't think she anticipated that I, as the eight-year-old winner, would ask for the adult magazine, *Archaeology*. In an effort to keep my mind engaged, my father began to take me with him when he drove to quarterly meetings at the main State Parks office in Raleigh. Handing me change for a drink and snack, he would drop me off at the NC Museum of Art or the Museum of Natural History and I would happily spend the day exploring the exhibits until it was time to meet him at the entrance for the long ride home.

My mother was more concerned with making me socially acceptable and faithful. A devout Methodist, she took us to a nearby country church. Although my father occasionally accompanied us to please her, he made it clear that he felt closer to God in Nature.

I can remember hiking together and his pointing to a nearby oak. "That's God being a tree," he explained, and his finger shifted to the cumulus clouds that towered above us. "And that's God being clouds." His gesture encompassed the landscape around us. "God's everywhere, especially in nature."

His perspective undoubtedly contributed to my Animism. Around the age of nine, I began to ask awkward questions of my Sunday School teachers. My inclination to challenge doctrine led the church elders to declare me disruptive and unwelcome, which ultimately ended my relationship with Methodism.

During the busy summer season, it was common for my father to work 70 hours a week. Since our home phone was also the park's phone, he was often called away to search for lost Boy Scouts or to deal with drunk campers. His responsibilities as superintendent left little time for shared family activity. Ongoing conflicts between my parents spilled over as they projected their own body image issues onto me and hounded me about my weight, pressuring me to be more compliant and conventional.

In the midst of our family conflicts, music seemed to bring us together. My parents were early stereo aficionados with a huge collection of recordings, and I was exposed to everything from Balinese Gamelan to Mozart to Jacobean ballads. On Saturday afternoons, I would sit by my mother as she knitted on her current project, and we would listen to the radio broadcast of the Metropolitan Opera. Pop played the guitar and harmonica, both with some skill. On summer evenings after he'd patrolled the park and locked the gate, we often all sat on the patio singing folk songs together. I eventually took up the guitar and studied voice. To this day, my deep, resonant alto is one of the primary shamanic tools I use to call power and honor my Gods, Ancestors, and spirits.

The forests, fields, streams, and mountains of the park became my refuge, filled with wonders and populated with many other Beings, none of whom judged me. I came home from school each afternoon, did my chores, and vanished into the woods until suppertime. In a field where deer often grazed, I would lie on my back and watch the Red Tail Hawks that nested in a big loblolly pine soar and play, keening their joy into the blue sky. Over their calls, I heard the quiet rustle of the deer moving in the long grass, often calling them closer to me by mimicking their sounds. I knew the bare patches where rains exposed arrowheads and followed the veins of white quartz boulders, turning over those that I sensed might hold pockets of sparkling crystals. As I wandered those woods, I made up songs to the rocks and plants and animals and built little temples for the fairy spirits that lived along my favorite stream. I was bullied by no one and could safely open all my senses without fear of being overwhelmed by the pain of others. In doing so, I came to realize that the world was filled with Beings rather than with things.

When my mother asked what I did during my long hours wandering the woods, I told her, "I'm singing to the North Wind."

In curious recurrent dreams, I was a large black and gold spotted cat, lazing high above the rainforest floor on a wide branch or hunting in humid jungles. At that age, I didn't know the difference between jaguars and leopards — or that the former are feared and revered throughout Central and South America as the protectors of shamans or as those shamans in their animal form. These dreams were to form the basis for my life-long love of cats and for the alliance I am honored to share with Mother Jaguar, who has no place in the traditions of the North but aids me nonetheless.

The world was also filled with voices — some the thoughts of others, some from the Dead. I would sometimes experience past events associated with a location as if watching a film clip unroll. Occasionally, an object told me a piece of its story: I would feel the old man who'd once owned a particular pocket watch or the despair that clung to an antique mirror my mom purchased. When I visited my cousin, I was always fearful about getting up during the night to use the bathroom across the upstairs hall because I sensed a "ghost" in the front bedroom. It was only years later that I learned her paternal grandmother had died a hard and lingering death from cancer there and that my cousin's family all avoided going into that room.

My knack for finding things often led me to clumps of crystals and other treasures. I would picture the item in my mind and simply "know" where to look. Often, something compelled me to walk to a place, and I would find something of note. While searching through a heap of chips and flakes left behind by the ancient residents of the area in their tool-making process, I had a vision of a dark green-gray projectile point of an unusual shape, delicate, with serrated edges, a form very different from those commonly found in my area. I turned around and extended my arm to brace myself — and in doing so, I placed my hand on the exact stone point I had pictured.

Although I remained awkward with other kids, I had a rapport with animals and dreamed of owning a horse. Among the neighbors living near the park was a family with horses and ponies. I began to visit as often as possible, cleaning tack, shoveling stalls, and eventually being allowed to ride. I slept, ate, and breathed horses, making pocket money at school by selling the detailed drawings I produced of them. Horse became the symbol of the freedom and power I longed for.

When I tried to ask my mother about the eerie things I sensed and experienced, her response was adamant. "You have too much imagination," I was told over and over, as if such a thing was possible or would make the world unsafe for me. It was a code phrase that actually meant, "That isn't real." It was a phrase that undermined my reality and left me wondering constantly where I belonged.

Four
SHADOW AND LIGHT

As the youngest of six, born to Victorian parents, my father struggled with how to relate to his children, especially me, his first born. He had been taught to show his love for his family by providing for us, but, like many men of his generation, struggled with any sort of emotional intimacy. His pay as a park superintendent was minimal, and family finances were a common source of conflict between my parents, but their resourcefulness provided us with beautiful hand-made clothing and toys and simple, hearty meals.

My happiest memories of him are of the times he took me exploring in the park's wilderness, showing me Nature's wonders as if revealing his own personal treasures. I recall lying beside him on a pad of scratchy woolen Army blankets in the bed of the park's pickup truck, looking up at the night sky as he pointed out and named constellations and their primary stars or climbing the steep slope of the mountain behind our house to collect "lightwood," the hard, resinous knots left behind as large, fallen pines rotted away. When split into sharp splinters, they perfumed the house with their turpentine fragrance and helped ignite the fires he loved to build in our small fireplace on chilly winter mornings.

Between the long hours he worked and my mother's need for a break from my challenging younger brother, there were few occasions when it was just my father and I. I recall the early spring morning he awakened me well before dawn and helped me dress, driving up one of the park's winding gravel fire trails to park and climb silently through the frosty woods. We crouched behind boulders, and he pointed out the shadowed recess of a fox den. When the vixen emerged to hunt, we carefully approached, and he let me peek into the recess to see her tiny, squirming pups.

Another magical day, he hooked up a motor to one of the park's aluminum rowboats and we played "pirate," exploring the ramshackle fish shacks scattered around Lake Tillery in a hunt for treasure. Lunch consisted of salty saltine crackers, a can of sardines, and a crisply sweet apple deftly peeled in one continuous strip with his razor-sharp pen knife. My prize of the day was a glossy black stone knife, knapped by some native resident thousands of years before and worn to silky smoothness by the water's action. I have and treasure it still.

Although it was never said, I knew my father regretted that his first-born wasn't a son — perhaps unaware of the quirk of genetics that had placed me closer to that role than others realized. I was bold, resourceful, fiercely independent: qualities that pleased him. However, when, thanks to the CAH, I entered early puberty and began to look like a girl, he was no longer quite sure how to relate to me, and our connection became more conflicted. I suspect that I reminded him of the older sisters who raised him, not always kindly, and he came to be unjustly critical of me. Meantime, as my brother grew into a boy who could toss a football or join my father in his other obsession, lifting weights, their bond strengthened.

As Reid and I grew, my mother realized that she needed a cause apart from us to give meaning to her life. Having personally experienced the lack of area mental health resources, she reached out to a couple of local physicians, and together they approached community business leaders, seeking financial support to establish a community clinic. Determined that others not suffer as she had, Mom lobbied the state legislature and eventually the governor. North Carolina was woefully behind the times in the care offered to mentally ill residents. Her efforts helped to bring about a modern mental health care system in North Carolina and the establishment of a local community mental health center where she led support groups for patients returning home from hospitalization.

Her commitment to progressive, compassionate mental health care and emphasis on the helpfulness of therapy led to my commitment to work on my own issues with skilled counselors, as I strongly encourage my students of the Northern Traditions to do. While we may have no control over the traumas that we experience, we are most certainly responsible for who we become in response to them. These traumas may sensitize us and thus make us more useful to the Holy Powers as healers and diviners. Still, we are responsible for learning to thrive in our lives, something only possible when we recognize that coping strategies that may have once made trauma survivable may later impair our ability to be fully present and engaged.

My mother's personal struggle toward wholeness also helped to shape me. While I was regarded by my classmates as bright and gifted, I was also an outsider. Perhaps that status conferred with it the sense that I was somehow safe to entrust with secrets, safe to come out to. I only know that from an early age, I found myself in the role of confidante and counselor to those who, like myself, were marginalized.

As I entered my teens, a growing sense of spiritual calling built in me, although at the time, there were no opportunities for women as clergy. This "calling" led to friendship with the young priest at the local Episcopal Church, and his kind counsel and lack of judgment offered acceptance, wisdom, and encouragement. I found myself drawn to the beauty of ritual and the sense of sacred mystery tangible in the Anglican *Book of Common Prayer* compared with the stark, almost business-like services in my childhood church. Hoping to make sense of the disjunction between my own experiences and the reality others seemed to believe in, I began reading about mysticism and the spiritual traditions of the ancient world.

By that time, the Vietnam War was well underway, and many young men either fled the country or sought exemption from the draft. The summer of my junior year of high school, I volunteered at a camp for handicapped children held at a Quaker boarding school and developed a friendship with a young man doing service there as a conscientious objector. He introduced me to his mother, the school cook, who immediately recognized me as a fellow "sensitive." Over the course of several evenings, she explained about ESP, Extra Sensory Perception, and taught me about the human energy field as well as how to shield myself psychically. For the first time, I felt seen and acknowledged by someone who understood the burden of experiencing the world in such an overwhelming way.

By the mid-1960s, in the cotton-mill town near the park, a few adventurous young people were beginning to smoke pot. I started hanging out with a group of older kids and occasionally got high, making pocket money by performing in several rock bands and by selling the brass hippie jewelry I'd started making. The massacre at Kent State my senior year fueled my inner fire; I became an activist, marching in demonstrations against the war. A friend had given me a deck of Tarot cards, and I found I was able to use my sensitivity to work with the graphic symbols quite readily. This led to my giving readings to curious classmates and acquaintances that they often found disquietingly accurate.

As I approached high school graduation, it was apparent my dream of becoming an archaeologist wasn't going to happen. "We can't afford for you to go to that college out west," my father declared. "Why can't you just study a normal woman's profession? Be a nurse, or a teacher, or a secretary?"

I adamantly declined, and my dad shook his head in frustration. "Then you'll just have to attend an in-state school, and maybe find some way to use your artistic talent commercially."

At 17, I became the second woman to be accepted into the Architecture program at the North Carolina State University School of Design in Raleigh. While I was excited at the prospect of moving away from my controlling parents, I already grieved the coming loss of sanctuary my beloved woods afforded. As the nights warmed, I often quietly removed the screen from my bedroom window, tossed my rolled-up sleeping bag to the ground, climbed down and wandered into the forest until I came to a welcoming spot. Nestled against a tree, I curled up, confident in my safety, and slept until the birdsongs signaled the coming day, cueing me to return to my family home. I did not understand that I was already struggling with my history of trauma.

Attending a large university in the state capitol could have been exhilarating had I not been crippled by depression and social anxiety. Nothing in my life had prepared me for the change of environment from quiet woods to busy city and busier campus. I began by attending the second semester of summer school, in order to meet the math requirements. The shy girl who had no gift for small talk and had never had a close friend found herself living in a huge high-rise dormitory. Unaware that I had a learning disability involving mathematics called dyscalculia, I struggled with and failed algebra but aced an elective graduate-level class in the History of Architecture.

It was at about this time that I had my first encounter with psychedelics. A friend had somehow obtained and gifted me with a dose of clinically pure mescaline, the active ingredient in the small, round peyote cactus long held as sacred by

Native Americans. Having some innate sense that this was not something to be approached as casual recreation, I held the small white tablet until the fall semester. It was then, on a warm September night, that I asked a young man I trusted to be my "sitter" and trip companion. Unlike his housemates, who were casually knocking back hits of LSD with Rum-and-Coke to the music of Jimi Hendricks and King Crimson, Tom insisted we enter into the experience reverently. He led me into his poster-adorned room, where we sat facing one another, lit a candle, and prayed to be given a good journey.

"You'll be fine," he assured me. "I'll stay right with you." He handed me a glass of water and smiled as I swallowed the key to a whole new universe. "Let's go up where it's quieter," he suggested and so we made our way, blankets in hand, to the shallow, sloping roof of the building.

For the next six hours I lay transfixed as complex geometric patterns in luminous colors danced across the inner landscape of my mind. The stars above us gyred in arabesques and the universe was filled with all the choirs of heaven.

Tom held my hand and patiently reassured me when the experience became overwhelming. "Hey, you're ok. It's beautiful, right? Just go with it. Just float in the beauty."

The sense of Oneness with all creation which I experienced that night has remained with me ever after, along with profound gratitude toward a gentle young man who understood the deep significance of such a sacrament.

The business and psychic noise of city and university life overwhelmed me. By the fall semester, I was floundering, often too depressed to get out of bed for my classes. That winter, unbeknown to my parents, I dropped out of college and rented a tiny room from some friends who lived just off campus. For some time I'd helped support myself by making art. I sold paintings and designed, sewed, and embroidered funky hippie clothing for "head shops" and boutiques, but most commercially successful was the rustic jewelry I forged and fabricated, often based on primitive designs from my archaeology books.

Inevitably, my parents learned of my circumstance and insisted that I return home to get sorted out. A friend had told me about Penland School of Crafts, located in the Black Mountains of North Carolina, and I talked my parents into allowing me to use some of the money set aside for my education so that I could take a class in metalsmithing.

At 18, I was the youngest person attending the school at that time. There, in the metals shop, I learned to work with silver — icy, malleable, and luminous — piercing the shining sheets with a hair-thin jeweler's saw before forging and forming elements I soldered together with an oxy-acetylene torch. I learned basic stone setting and my experiments with lost-wax casting convinced me that I preferred an architectural approach, that of fabrication and construction. By the time I returned home later that summer, I knew I would be a jeweler — one of several careers I was to pursue in which I was not required to "act like a girl."

After several rocky months, I moved into my first apartment and began working part-time at a local jewelry store, learning to size rings and do simple repairs at the bench with their in-house jeweler. I'd managed to acquire a few files, several pairs of jeweler's pliers, a ball-peen hammer, and a jeweler's saw frame. My soldering was accomplished with a clumsy plumber's propane torch. I'd come back from Penland with a small collection of semi-precious gemstones and using my primitive tools, set about finding my style as an art jeweler.

I also experienced my first profound precognitive event, sensing the moment when my beloved paternal grandmother died of a heart attack. Knowing that my mother would be coming to tell me, I showered, put on an appropriate dress, and packed my suitcase, astonishing my mother and the minister who accompanied her when they arrived.

Following my grandmother's death, my father, who had always struggled with highs and lows, grew increasingly unstable, often drinking too much, and finally taking early retirement from State Parks under his doctor's orders. He and my mother bought a rambling old farmhouse on a bend of the New River in the rugged mountains of Ashe County and settled into restoring it and putting in a garden. They were content together for the first time in decades.

In order to have any hope of supporting myself, I decided I needed to move to a more urban area where my jewelry might find more of a market, and so I returned to Raleigh because it was already familiar to me. Knowing my income would be unpredictable, I took whatever part-time jobs I could find doing alterations and cleaning houses, making jewelry at the small table in my kitchen in my off hours.

Friends I had known during my short stint in college had become active in a medieval reenactment group, the Society for Creative Anachronism or SCA, and encouraged me to attend a couple of events. I loved the idea of creating a historical persona for myself and immediately began my research. With no hesitation, I created a character drawn from the horse people of the Central Asian steppe. At the time, most folks based their characters on medieval Europe, so this seemed an odd choice. In retrospect, it was also a prescient one.

My life began to fall into place. For the next several years, I concentrated on building my skills at a craft I was increasingly passionate about and discovered that my old love of archaeology, myths, and legends gave me a vocabulary from which to design. While not literal reproductions of historical jewelry, the pieces I was creating certainly drew inspiration from those intricate, magical jewels I first came to love during the many hours I spent wandering museums.

1973 proved a breakthrough year. After multiple attempts, I was juried into the Piedmont Crafts Guild, a prestigious organization of top Southeastern artisans. Pieces of my work were selected for exhibitions at the North Carolina Museum of Art and the Southeastern Center for Contemporary Art. Caught up in the first wave of the wearable art movement, I was inspired to create elaborate personal ornaments combining tribal and Art Nouveau elements. My customers often remarked on how healing and empowering they found them, helping me to recognize I was putting in something more than unusual materials and good design.

That fall, I participated in the large, regional Piedmont Crafts Fair for the first time, feeling both honored to be included and wholly out of my depth. Perhaps recognizing my "deer in the headlights" look, a fiber artist named Marea Streat took me under her wing, calming me with mugs of tea and her grounding presence. Her kind and loving encouragement formed the foundation for an enduring friendship and opened the door into the beautiful and diverse realm of the fiber arts, many of which I use today in my own life and shamanic practice. Also deeply intuitive, Marea offered affirmation in my spiritual and personal journey when my own mother could not. Our rapport was such that I came to refer to her as my "Other Mother," and our friendship remains an enduring blessing in my life.

Uncannily, useful things found their way to me. At a time when I struggled to afford materials to work with, a friend whose grandfather had been a lapidary gifted me with a bag of colorful agates and jaspers he had cut and polished that were perfect for accenting cuffs, earrings, and pendants.

I was stopped on the street one day by an unfamiliar young man. "You make jewelry, right?"

I nodded.

"I've got something for you. I thought you might be able to do something with these..." He led me across the street to his truck and pulled out a beautiful pair of deer antlers. I'd been invited two weeks previously to participate in a wearable art exhibition and was struggling with what to submit. The antlers proved to have the perfect curvature to form a dramatic neckpiece when I hinged them butt-to-butt, and the piece was subsequently featured in publicity for the show.

Another person brought me a box containing antique mastodon ivory bracelets, piano key ivories, and slices of walrus ivory. There was something especially magical about working with these organic materials, and I experimented with carving, inlay, and scrimshaw, the latter technique often featuring primitive images reminiscent of Paleolithic cave paintings of shamanic figures with antler crowns and big-bellied Goddesses.

Art and spirit were coming together.

Season Two

Preparation, Spring

Days lengthen and shoots emerge from melting snow,
Tender and swollen with possibility.
The warming forest is astir,
In promise of the land's awakening.
Birdsongs ring out in courtship,
Flower-colors taking wing as
All are called to couple.
On warming afternoons, sap rises and
Tree-frogs trill their chorus of desire:
Pick me! Pick me!
Amid the dappled light and shadow
Of her hidden bower,
A doe strains and pushes forth
Twin fawns: sleek, wet, and gasping,
All long legs and wonderment.
I, too, emerge to drink the light,
Turning my face like a sunflower
Toward brightness.
Probing warming earth, I lay my seeds in tidy rows
And pray for rain,
Already dreaming of October's bounty.

 *Five*

CONSPICUOUS

Extensive childhood trauma and my parents' constant discounting of my perceptions undermined my confidence in my
instincts and compromised my ability to recognize potentially
problematic people. I had been taught to be compliant and
had never learned how to define or hold healthy boundaries.
My conditioning taught me to focus on being helpful, not discerning, resulting in a series of unhealthy relationships.

In 1976, at an event hosted by the Society for Creative
Anachronism, I met W., a young biochemistry major who was
intense, brilliant, and as passionate about music, history, and
mysticism as I was. I was 23 and lonely. My housemates had
recently moved out, and I needed help making my rent; my
friend needed a place to live where he could have his cats. He
moved in, and we became lovers. To stave off the disapproval
of our parents, it seemed logical to get married; so, we announced our engagement at Christmas, despite their opposi-
tion.

The following summer, we were wed in my folks' front
yard. When we returned from a week of camping in the
mountains, I was surprised to receive a job offer for a full-
time teaching position at a community arts center in the foothills of the Blue Ridge. The position offered a regular income
and the opportunity for me to develop my style further as a
metalsmith. I didn't hesitate. We packed my VW Beetle with
belongings and cats and drove northwest to Wilkes County, a
mountainous area in the northwestern corner of North Carolina long famed for stock car racing and moonshine. There, we
rented a tiny house in the equally tiny community of Cricket.

In such a rural, conservative place, my long-haired and

bearded husband found employment elusive. Each morning, I left for the Arts Center, having no idea how he spent his days. Although I worked long hours, often teaching evening classes, he proved critical and demanding, still expecting me to cook and clean. I began to suspect I'd erred in my choice of partner, as he veered from emotionally remote to explosive.

The situation grew even more complicated when I discovered that he also enjoyed casual encounters with other men. I had known many gay men and had deep friendships with a few, but I wanted a husband who cherished me, whom I could trust, and with whom I felt safe. My efforts at trying to talk about these issues with him were met by stony silence or threatening outbursts. I'd made a terrible mistake but felt trapped by messages from my family that they had, after all, warned me, and I would just have to make the best of my marriage as my mother had with my father.

I focused on the classes I was teaching and on creating adornments for clients and galleries — anything to generate income. Sharing a workplace with other progressive, creative people offered fellowship, and I soon learned that one of my Arts Center co-workers had long studied mysticism and had an interest in shamanism, having encountered it during a time in Southeast Asia. "You have The Sight," Lee said, "and you put something special, something magical in your jewelry. I can feel it, and people who buy your work will feel it, too."

With his instruction, I began to see how my Gift could be harnessed and used to benefit others. He also taught me about the runes (Proto-Norse: ᚱᚢᚾᛟ = *runo*, Old Norse: *rún*), a set of related alphabets used to write various Germanic languages and possibly adapted from the Latin alphabet. Rune-like symbols appear as cave markings as early as the late Bronze Age. The earliest runic inscriptions date from the second century C.E., but their use in ritual and as an oracle for consultation must certainly pre-date their use as a system of writing. While most practitioners use 24 characters, a 33-character form is also used. Each rune is associated with a particular spirit, and, in order to work with them in depth, one must cultivate a reciprocal relationship with them, as with any other Being. One use of the runes is in *galdr*, a process of intoning the name of a rune in such a way as to engage with and direct the spirit of that specific rune. *Galdr* can be used to heal, to cleanse, to invoke, to curse, and to bless. Rune sets are traditionally carved in discs or slats of wood, with certain woods associated with specific runes. Other materials include clay, stone, and even bone.

During slow times at the Arts Center, Lee taught me how to meditate and, then, how to enter a trance state. In that altered consciousness, accessed through rhythmic breathing patterns, I found I could sense qualities present in various precious metals and gemstones, creating jewelry that brought their spirits together in ways people remarked on.

"Your work almost feels alive," one woman exclaimed.

"I never take my pendant off," said another. "It makes me feel grounded, focused."

With encouragement, my jewelry designs increasingly drew from ancient sacred imagery, intentionally combining art and magic. I have no doubt that the knowledge and skills my colleague shared formed the foundation for my subsequent work in the Northern Traditions.

When funding for my position at the Art Center eventually ran out, W. and I moved to the village of East Bend, located in the foothills near the artsy tobacco town of Winston Salem where I'd been born. My husband continued commuting to musical activities with a regional orchestra, where he played violin, and to his job as a pharmacy tech. I divided my time between my jewelry work and work in a picture frame shop cutting mats, stretching needlework, and assembling frames. Eventually, after several years, W. was accepted at the School of Pharmacy at the University of North Carolina. We moved to Chapel Hill, and I continued making jewelry, working multiple jobs to pay the bills. As a "hippie" artist-type, I felt at liberty to dress in jeans and soft cotton shirts, fabrics I found soothing, gender-neutral, and more aligned with my inner sense of self.

That December, I was stunned to find myself pregnant, despite having an IUD. Knowing how W. felt about children, I'd never anticipated becoming a mom. I was excited but also terrified of the financial implications. In February, my ever-intuitive mother sent me a Valentine card wishing her love to me and "one or two more." I was puzzled. Six weeks later, during a routine checkup on April Fool's Day of 1981, an ultrasound revealed that I was carrying twins. My mind reeled — how would we possibly manage? By May, my obstetrician was concerned that I might be at risk of going into labor prematurely and placed me on bed rest. With me unable to work and no money coming in, we were in for a tough time. Our families, both several hours away, were of little help. W. spent most of his waking hours on campus, trying to get through school as quickly as possible.

During this time, I was to meet the woman who has remained my dearest and most enduring friend. Kristy and I both experienced a sure sense that we had known one another in some prior lifetime; without her help and love, I'm not sure how I would have coped. In late July, after a long and difficult labor, my beautiful sons were born by caesarian. I count them among the great blessings of my life.

Following early graduation, W. found a position as a pharmacist in Winston Salem, and, in December of 1982, we moved once again. The emotional roller coaster now impacted not just me but two precious little boys. I was constantly on guard, doing my best to appease my husband, never knowing what would trigger his outbursts, and doing my best to deflect his outbursts from our boys. Two years later, I could no longer tolerate his abuse, and I asked him to move out.

As a single parent, I needed additional income, and the demands of my busy toddlers made metalsmithing very difficult. Once I managed to enroll my sons in daycare part-time, I commuted 45 minutes to work as a bench jeweler in a retail store.

I also supplemented my income through musical gigs. For years, I'd worked intermittently as a folk singer, playing at bars and clubs. I began playing as part of a Celtic duo called Tinker's Damn. My musical partner, Jack Ehrhardt, and I had known one another since our reenactment days, and his wife, Bobbie, provided much appreciated childcare. Between the two of us, Jack and I played guitar, the Irish bouzouki, Appalachian dulcimer, tin whistle, and the psaltery, accompanying a wide variety of songs and ballads from the British Isles. I loved performing — and doing so with Jack was magic. We played street fairs and opened for noted folk artists like Martin Carthy and the Breton band Kornog. We were even featured at North Carolina's quadricentennial celebration in Manteo, the tiny coastal town said to be the site of the Lost Colony. There, noted broadcaster Walter Cronkite and the CBS news crew filmed the event. Jack and I welcomed the historic sailing ship Queen Elizabeth II into the harbor with song, sweltering in heavy Elizabethan clothing in the 95 degree heat.

The financial struggles and emotional distress over my shattered marriage were compounded by unhealed trauma and depression. Overwhelmed and exhausted, I contemplated suicide, but my love and concern for my children kept me struggling on. Early the following year, feeling I had no choice, I allowed W. to move back home. In an effort to repair our relationship, we bought a house, and, at my insistence, began therapy. Neither helped. Issues with his infidelity and intermittent abuse continued.

One day in a bookstore, I picked up a copy of Starhawk's *The Spiral Dance*, a groundbreaking work combining eco-feminism and witchcraft. As I learned about this ancient religion that honored the Divine Feminine, something began to awaken deep within me. Through therapy, I had come to recognize that I carried a great deal of my father's internalized misogyny and my own inner discomfort with feeling male in a (somewhat) female body. In an effort to befriend the female part of myself, I developed a private personal spiritual practice based on honoring the Goddess and, in doing so, began to heal my relationship with my body. Realizing that I could only advance so far on my own, I prayed to the Goddess to help me find a teacher knowledgeable in Women's Mysteries.

In the spring of 1987, a wealthy collector of my work invited me to help plan a public Beltane celebration at the spiritual center she owned, where I happened to meet Mary, a High Priestess in the Gardnerian Tradition of English Witchcraft. In the weeks following the Beltane ceremony, several of us committed to forming our own tiny coven and began to meet on a regular basis. Mary had a son the same age as my boys, and they often played in another room as we gathered in Circle to learn the Old Ways of our wise foremothers.

In those days, the lore was still oath-bound and highly secretive, still in the "broom closet." During those occasions, Mary taught us about this rich spiritual practice honoring both the Divine Feminine and the Divine Masculine, and I began to understand that I could carry and honor both within myself. We learned to dance and sing ourselves into an ecstatic state, to gather life force energy from the world around us, and, then, to intentionally direct it toward a goal. This is the foundation of magic: the use of will to alter reality. I found that the exercises we shared helped strengthen and stabilize my innate psychic gifts and also gave me newfound courage, self-worth, and motivation.

My sons started pre-K, finally allowing me time to work on weekdays between 9:00 a.m. and 2:00 p.m. After a fellow metalsmith and I rented studio space together in a drafty warehouse, I began to rebuild my jewelry business. The following spring, in Winston Salem's infant Arts District, I opened Jewels of the Spirit, a tiny shop featuring my work. Located above a pottery studio, the bright corner space with its tall windows and high ceiling brought me joy and healing, while giving me time apart from my boys and my husband's controlling presence to begin making friends and forming professional connections. Here, I had a space of my own where I could create and experiment to my own choice of music amid a community of fellow craftsmen. Monthly gallery hops brought a flow of potential new customers and blossoming confidence.

Using skills I'd learned from my magical studies, I learned to drop into what some researchers have termed the "flow state," and which I thought of as the "Maker's Trance," which I later wrote about in my 2019 work, *The Duergarbok: The Dwarves of the Northern Tradition*:

> For me, just accessing the part of my brain where my creative process resides carries with it a different sort of consciousness: I lose all sense of time and awareness of things around me, apart from what I am focused on. My thinking becomes spiral rather than linear or sequential. While I transition readily into this right-brain mode, I find it much more difficult to shift back to everyday, left-brain consciousness. (Normally, I am capable of remembering what my pantry

contains and can readily improvise a meal, but when I've been in "studio brain," forget about me being able to pull together an impromptu dinner. "Studio" or Right Brain is also relatively non-verbal for me.) Humming, chanting or singing along with recorded music also deepens this trance-like creative state. There have been many occasions when I "came to" to find some rather remarkable object before me and had no idea how I made it or how it got there.

Around this time, the coven I was part of was asked to take over the planning and presentation of public full Moon ceremonies at Wellsprings—celebrations that were well attended despite hostile demonstrations and threats from several local Baptist churches. Wellsprings also hosted workshops by practitioners of many other faiths and traditions, and these afforded me my first formal shamanic training in the Q'ero tradition of the Andes.

On my 37th birthday, W. gave me a cutting of the sacred San Pedro cactus – *Echinopsis pachanoi* – used as a medicine plant by the shamans of Peru. Also known as the Cactus of the Four Winds, the plant is considered valuable as a teaching spirit and ally. I potted up the stout green stem and placed it by my side of the bed where the afternoon Sun could warm it, curious to see whether the lore that the spirit of the plant could teach through dreams was true.

The San Pedro cutting must be rooting. For several nights, I've experienced a series of powerful shamanic dreams in which I "fly" south over the Isthmus of Panama to the upper reaches of the Am-

*azon where I encounter an old native man painted like a jaguar
who takes me into the rainforest and teaches me to recognize many
healing plants and sing their spirit songs. Last night, in the midst of
a forest clearing, I sat with him on a huge rock.*

*We were soon joined by another teacher spirit, a Being as much
plant as man. The two winked at each other, laughing at my desire to
learn the "Green Magic."*

Plantman asked, "Are you willing to be conspicuous?"

*Before I could respond, he reached across to mark my chin with a
distinctive tattoo.*

Conspicuous — the very thing my parents feared I would be.
To access magic and power, was I willing to be seen as who
I truly am? A healer, an intersex person, a psychically gifted
person, and someone who walks many worlds? I eventually
came to understand that being conspicuous is a fundamental
part of serving as a shaman.

My life remained very difficult, and I dealt with my sense
of vulnerability in the only way I knew — by self-calming with
food as I had seen my mother do. I lay awake at night, wondering when my husband would explode again, never knowing what would trigger a scathing attack or a blow, always
feeling wrong — too much and not enough. In an exhausting
pattern reminiscent of what I experienced with my father, I
found myself trying to anticipate what would trigger W.'s
outbursts in hopes of placating him.

HIV was epidemic in the mid-80s, and, knowing his pref-
erences, I was terrified. I knew that I wanted a divorce, but
experience had shown me that he was likely to be vindictive.
My craftsman's income was unpredictable and clearly insuffi-

cient for me to provide for myself and my boys. How could I possibly manage to make a new life for us?

I wept silently, praying to the Gods and spirits I had come to revere for help and courage.

Six
GIFTS

I am convinced that the Holy Powers heard my prayers. In the spring of 1989, I was contacted by Wake Forest University and engaged to design and create an elaborate silver, gold, and onyx ceremonial Chain-of-Office to be worn by their Chancellor. The commission was the largest of my career up to that point, and the university advanced funds for the project, making possible other major life changes.

Friends encouraged me to attend massage school so that I would have a professional umbrella under which to practice the intuitive shamanic work and spiritual counseling I had begun offering in addition to my metalwork. This made sense as it would also provide me with additional income necessary for me to leave my marriage. In September of 1990, I enrolled at the Body Therapy Institute near Chapel Hill. At the time, I was operating Jewels of the Spirit, working part-time at Wellsprings as a program director, and commuting from Winston Salem to massage school three nights a week and every other weekend. I rose at 5 a.m., did chores and packed my sons' lunches, dropped them off at school at 7:30 a.m., drove to my shop or to Wellsprings, worked until 4 p.m., drove the 90 minutes to massage school, attended class from 7 p.m. to 10 p.m., then drove home to fall into bed. If I'd had any idea of how difficult that year would be, I'm not sure I would have attempted it.

My massage training included extensive education in anatomy and physiology. It was during this time that I realized that my body was clearly atypical. I began to suspect that I might have some sort of genetic anomaly impacting my genitals and my sense of gender. I also happened to see a documentary on intersex individuals presenting as female that resonated with my own experience. When I worked magically with my energy body, it always appeared to me as male, but, prior to that point, I had no frame of reference for being simultaneously male and female.

That autumn, the coven's "Wicca 101" weekly introductory classes were well attended. Among the inquirers was a young IT engineer named Eric who impressed me with his quiet steadiness and deep knowledge of myths and lore. We also shared a deep sense of familiarity. The concept of reincarnation is a significant part of my belief system, and I have often met individuals in this lifetime I am certain I have known in others. This was the case with Eric. When I moved my jewelry shop around the corner to a more accessible location in a street-level artists' co-op, he showed up to wrestle heavy display cases, anvils, and boxes of hammers. He began to stop by at lunchtime, bringing sandwiches and welcome company; we dined on gyros from the local Greek restaurant and talked magic and mythology. Having been so long treated with disdain or ignored, his kindness was a balm to my soul.

One evening, following a sweat lodge at Wellsprings at which Eric had served as fire tender, an event was to occur that proved a wake-up call. I'd returned the estate's golf cart, which we'd used to haul supplies, to the garage and was closing up when the door slipped, crushing my fingertips between the louvers. Trapped and in pain, I screamed for help. Eric came running to my aid while my husband sat in the car up the hill and later berated me for being so stupid. The contrast was eye-opening.

Gradually, the friendship between Eric and me became more. In his sea-blue eyes, I saw respect and genuine love, and his touch was tender and protective. One afternoon as he visited with me in my workshop, I broke down, confessing my deep unhappiness. I clearly had a decision to make. Seeking guidance, I drove north to the breast-shaped peak of Pilot Mountain, long a sacred site, and there asked the Holy Powers for a sign. As I sat in prayer late into the summer evening, ravens, seen as spirit messengers by Native Americans and the Norse, soared and called over me — ultimately gifting me with a feather as a sign to step forward into a life of my own.

After graduating from BTI in July, I informed W. that I needed some time to myself to sort things out. I rented a small house, and, like most women escaping abusive marriages, took the absolute minimum I needed: a few pieces of furniture, my guitars, and the art and craft items I had created or traded my work for. A friend gave me her old couch, and the house had come with a kitchen table. I slept on a second-hand mattress on the floor. I can recall feeling guilty over wanting a new life and thinking that if I took very little, perhaps W. would be less angry.

Still, awakening each morning in a space filled with peace and sunlight, I felt immense relief and a new sense of freedom. I was able to support myself with income from my jewelry business and bodywork appointments, supplemented by the funds I'd squirreled away from the Wake Forest project. My sons alternated weeks with me and their father, who initially helped out, assuming that I would decide to come home. I began to heal.

The following February, Eric and I moved in together and found we were very compatible. From the beginning of our relationship, I had emphasized that my children and my spiritual life would always come first. To my surprise, Eric expressed the desire to support me and my sacred work, which was something I'd never experienced before. The boys continued alternate weeks with us and their dad, and Eric began building his own relationship with my energetic nine-year-olds.

Eric loved me as I was, perceiving me as female but respecting that was not how I thought of myself. That he never felt the need to confine me to any sort of socially defined identity allowed me the liberty to explore who I felt comfortable being. When the co-op building where my studio was located began to experience break-ins, I closed my shop and set up a studio in the garage at home. There was also a spare room for me to continue seeing bodywork clients.

One evening, I was giving Eric a massage; he often experienced stress headaches and we'd found that bodywork helped him to relax. The room was dark, apart from a single candle near the foot of the massage table and soft Celtic harp music was playing. As was often my practice in doing bodywork, I closed my eyes and allowed my hands to sense and read the contours beneath them. My work brought me to the head of the table and I prepared to place light traction on his neck.

Through slitted eyelids, I saw his body limned in candlelight and abruptly flashed back to another lifetime, when I stood, preparing to bathe the corpse of my beloved husband. Memories flooded in: of our shared life at a small croft in the highlands of Scotland, of his determination to join our clansmen in their ill-advised stand with Bonny Prince Charlie at the battle of Culloden, and of how his brothers brought his mutilated body home. I began to sob uncontrollably, flooded by memories and grief. Eric understood.

That summer I informed W. that I wanted a divorce and, as I had anticipated, any cooperation vanished, quickly to be followed by threats. Collecting child support grew more and more difficult, and, eventually, I received a letter from his attorney informing me of his intent to sue for custody on the basis I was an "unfit mother."

The following spring, Eric and I bought a home and continued building a life together. I began partnering with several therapists in town, doing bodywork by referral for their clients with histories of trauma — work in which my psychic gifts proved especially helpful.

In the face of trauma, we enter one of three states: Fight, Flight, or Freeze. Often traumatic events are managed by freezing or sequestering the memory under muscular tension. I found that when I placed my hand over the area where my client had sequestered an experience, I could "see" that event as if watching a movie. I used my intuition and clairsentience along with a combination of polarity therapy, energetic healing, and conventional massage techniques. In retrospect, I suppose I was trying to heal my own trauma by helping others to heal. From early childhood, I had been taught to be of service to others, and I had watched as my mother processed her own traumas through helping and counseling others.

As I began to align my life and sense of calling, uncanny gifts continued to flow. One of the gem dealers I purchased stones from handed me a small package when I finished making my selections. "Something told me you're going to need these one day," he said.

I unwrapped the contents to find two remarkable quartz crystals, one water-clear, slender and about seven inches long. The other, a gem-quality amethyst the size of my forefinger, carried within its purple depths the phantom pattern left as it formed within a void deep in the earth, grew, and formed again. Little did I know I would one day use them in a life-transforming ceremony in far-off Scotland.

During an outdoor show, a fellow jewelry exhibitor of Native American heritage, knowing I shared his interest in archaeology, presented me with a Choctaw medicine ball, a milk-white spherical stone about the size of a tennis ball long ago ground to a silky surface. I could immediately feel its age and power.

"The Old Ones used it for sucking out bad energy," he'd told me. "I thought you might be able to use it with those women you do healing on."

I brought the stone home and cleansed it with blessed saltwater. I was puzzled and enchanted by the fine-grained surface, almost skin-like, and then, astonished to discover that as I turned and warmed the stone in my hands, it "woke up" and became pliable, like the dense rubber of an artist's kneaded eraser.

One afternoon, I was working with a massage client suffering from a chronic muscle spasm in her back that I knew to be associated with childhood trauma. I asked whether she'd be open to me trying something new. We shared a strong connection, and, with her trust and permission, I warmed the medicine stone in my hands and began to roll it back and forth over the prominent knot beside her shoulder blade. "Let me know if it hurts," I advised her.

"Actually, that just feels nice and warm…"

I gently rocked the stone in small circles, intuitively collaborating with the tool. In a way that didn't make sense, it seemed to sink into the muscle. As I withdrew it, we both felt a sort of sucking.

"Did you hear that?" she asked. "That squelchy sound?"

I assured her that I had and noted that where there had been a lump on her back, there was now a shallow dip.

"It feels different — like you pulled something out."

Both of us were open but also skeptical. After the session, I cleansed the medicine stone again, leaving it to clear in salt and water, and, to my surprise, I returned later to find the liquid was the color of pale tea, a staining that could have come neither from the stone nor from its use on my client.

The client called the following morning, her excitement tangible. "Susannah — you'll never believe this but the spasm is gone, really gone. I slept through the night with no pain for the first time in months!"

In the years since, I've used the medicine stone many times. No matter how thoroughly I soak and scrub it prior to use, the water it is cleansed in afterwards is invariably tainted in a way I can't explain.

Between seeing bodywork clients, I gardened, sewed, painted, and made amazing jewelry. Eric and I set up a small greenhouse and studio in our back yard so that I would have a better workspace. My interest in shamanism and Indigenous healing grew stronger, and, soon, I was sharing my sunny studio with a variety of endangered rainforest plants, many of them strongly enspirited, filling the studio with their intoxicating perfumes. As I worked and sang to the plants, they began to sing back, drawing me into a collaborative relationship. I would slip into the Maker's Trance and "come to" hours later to find remarkable jewelry on my bench. This period generated some of my strongest work, an expression of my newfound happiness and flowering life.

I have come to understand that my early dreaminess helped me to survive a childhood where my lived reality was diametrically at odds with the reality everyone around me seemed to experience. The ability to "step sideways" from the many traumas in my life helped me to survive them and has ultimately proved to be an important skill for me as a shaman. The key has been learning how to manage that ability so that my use of it is intentional.

A friend recently asked me, "What is a trance and what happens when you go into one?"

I found this difficult to describe and I have no clue how my experiences compare with those of other practitioners, perhaps because there are different types of trance for different situations, and differing levels of dissociation are involved in each. On the most fundamental level, for me, it involves a softening of my focus and an opening to more subtle sources of information.

Imagine that you have left the busy city and driven up into the mountains. In your car, you are immersed in loud music from your radio, the scent of the coffee in your mug, the hum of the motor. Arriving at a trail head, you park your vehicle and wander down a trail into the forest. Your awareness grows more acute as you walk and you gradually begin to notice fresh sounds, smell new smells. You notice birdsongs, the splash of water, and perhaps the soft sigh of the wind. Breathing deeply, you smell moist earth and the spicy, resinous fragrance of the pines. Slowing down, you grow still and note the subtle impact of sun and shade, observing the tiny beings that play vital roles in the ecosystem: insects, fungi, invertebrates. You float in the deeper dance that is wild Nature, complex and rich. This is a bit like my experience of the trance state.

The Maker's Trance, that altered state of consciousness some researchers refer to as the Flow State, may have me so present in the process of creating that I lose all track of time and awareness unless a sharp stimulus interrupts me.

Song has long offered me ready access to another kind of altered state, particularly when combined with drumming or gentle swaying. The Gods and spirits I work with have often given me what some might call "Medicine Songs," and these have become a regular part of my practice, honoring the lighting of Fire or expressing gratitude to my Ancestors for their many gifts. The gift of song is part of sacred exchange. So, I offer gift songs before harvesting medicinal plants or when engaged in divination, desiring to balance the exchange with my allies. The Holy Powers have forged me to do this work, and it is right that I should use my voice to praise and honor Them.

Search Google for an image of a shaman, and, in all likelihood, you'll encounter a photo of someone playing a drum, perhaps the most ancient instrument. The rhythm of drumming entrains our heartbeat and our breath. It can be slow and meditative or carry us into a frenzy, changing the patterns of our brainwaves and entrancing us. I drum to journey, to manipulate energy, to remove problematic energies from clients and from "troubled" or haunted houses, a process jokingly referred to as "ghostbusting."

My intuitive gifts also express as another kind of trance, useful in divination, the art of using a mildly altered state of consciousness and tools such as Tarot cards or runes to gain insights for oneself or for a client in difficult circumstances. I discovered I had a knack for finding underground water sources, a skill known as dowsing. Traditional dowsing is often done using L-rods or Y-shaped branches as indicators of the target. I now understand this gift to be akin to a type of divination. I began doing land assessments and geomancy projects, often advising landowners on how to mend or improve the native energies of their property. It is a skill that still forms a significant portion of my shamanic practice.

I was called today to a rather grand Tudor-style home in an up-scale, older neighborhood. The owner — a well-dressed, conventional young woman in her early forties — suspected the house was haunted. It is my experience that this is rarely the case, but here I was wrong.

Commenting that her young daughter had grown afraid to sleep in her room due to nightmares and visions of what she'd described as "the dark boy," the woman led me upstairs to her child's room.

I could feel that something clearly wasn't right. Although there were tall leaded windows on two sides of the room, darkness gathered in the corners, next to the high ceiling. I explored there, then moved into the attached bathroom, with its original hexagonal tile floor and 1940s era fixtures. As I faced the mirror over the sink, the face of a gaunt youth looked back, mouth tight and eyes filled with pain. In a flash, the vision changed, and I saw the same young man suspended from the wrought iron light fixture overhead, his belt tight around his neck, his face swollen and discolored.

Numerous experiences had taught me that traumatic events can imprint on the energetic fabric of a location. After collecting myself, I used the supplies I'd brought and my skills to banish the sad presence of the boy from bath and bedroom, then made my way downstairs to speak with my client.

I asked her what she knew about the history of the house and she commented, "Not much, other than a neighbor mentioning that the original owner's son had committed suicide in one of the bathrooms upstairs."

Bingo! Such factual confirmation helps me to be more confident in my intuitive abilities. Still, as lovely as the house was, something else felt off. I asked to be shown the lower level of the home, which included unused servants' rooms, a buttery for the cold storage of produce, and dairy items and a large, L-shaped garage. Before ever setting foot in the garage, I could sense an angry presence. I asked my client to raise the garage door, which opened onto an empty driveway and backyard. Unlike the simple release of a tormented soul which I'd performed upstairs, this situation would prove a battle.

I had ritually "sealed" myself before starting work and took a minute to reinforce that spiritual armor. I set down the basket which held my blessed salt water, a clay censer with charcoal and a pungent banishing incense made of myrrh, dragon's blood and copal resins, and my lighter. The sense of fury was strongest in the blind end of the L; I steeled myself and stood there, opening my consciousness to see what I could sense.

As if watching a film, I found myself looking at the intersection of two colonial era trading paths. A heavily laden man approached, his back bowed beneath a heavy pack. Another man leapt from the bushes, knife in hand, flung the trader to the ground and swiftly cut his throat, robbing him of his goods.

This vision replayed over and over in my mind and I understood that the furious presence I faced was that of the murdered man whose blood had bound him to that very spot. I prayed and stated my intention to release the angry spirit. That was when I saw the first crows gathering in the yard behind me, first three or four, then more.

I proceeded with the ceremony to release the ghost and clear the negative energy left by his murder using salt water, smoke, and prayer. Each time I glanced back at the garage door, I could see more crows perched on the shrubs, on the swing set and on the lawn. As a final step, I made my way counterclockwise around the space, fanning the pungent yellowish-gray smoke into any spots holding negative residue and pushing that miasma ahead of me as if sweeping the floor. By then, the yard was dark with crows, perhaps as many as forty, and the eerie sight gave me goosebumps. As I pushed the last of the foul energy out the garage door, the crows abruptly took flight with a clatter of dark wings. Seriously strange stuff!

By night, my dreams were filled with vivid images of Paleolithic life: of cave paintings made with charcoal and red ochre by flickering torchlight, of the flowing gray-brown tide of a vast herd of reindeer, of sewing clothing made of deerskin, of consuming the red and white speckled caps of *Amanita* mushrooms to enter sacred trance.

Were they dreams or memories from other lifetimes?

I only knew that the dream images bled through into my creative life and appeared in the jewelry I made: big-bellied Goddesses swollen with possibility, antler-crowned forest lords, handprints, spirals. I taught myself to carve bone and fossil ivory using tiny, sharp jeweler's gravers and carved tiny masks and faces stained with earth pigments.

In addition to participating in Piedmont Craftsmen's gallery shows and annual fine crafts fairs, I sent work to exhibitions afar: New Orleans, Memphis, Salt Lake City, Arkansas, Michigan, and elsewhere. In particular, my traveling trunk show, "Ancient Artifacts and Sacred Symbols," was very successful. Many of the techniques I used are common among today's flood of art jewelers, but, in those days, their uniqueness made my work notable. While I accepted commissions for custom orders, I was happiest creating around my own visions, often finding inspiration in the remarkable collection of fossils and gemstones I'd gathered.

My life was richly productive, if not financially successful, but what was I? Wife and mother? Teacher, historian, frustrated amateur archaeologist? Naturalist, healer, spiritual counselor? Metalsmith, musician, psychic, crazy person? I only knew that the sense of calling that I felt colored and informed every aspect of my life.

I was ready to move on. Not long after my divorce was final-
ized, Eric proposed. We were married on May 1, 1994, on the
day the ancient Celts called Beltane and held sacred in celebration of the fertile, greening earth. It was a small gathering —
many of his buddies refused to attend, believing it to be some
sort of satanic ceremony — and my ex had actively alienated
most of my friends with his tales and lies. In the lush greenness of the outdoor lakeside chapel at Wellsprings, with Mary
and my musical partner Jack as our clergy and dear Kristy
as my attendant, we bound ourselves before the Gods and
jumped the broom into a shared life.

My jewelry business was also flowering. One of my bodywork clients, part of an international New Age spiritual group,
began to commission major pieces to be used in ceremonies
at sacred sites around the world. "Did you know that English
Heritage is reopening Stonehenge?" she asked me one day
after her massage.

I was aware the famed megalithic site had been closed to
ceremonial gatherings due to issues with vandalism.

"We've been invited to participate in the reconsecration,
and I want to commission a chalice from you for the ceremony. Is that something you could make?"

My eyes widened, and I assured her I could.

That evening I climbed the hill behind our house to sit
beneath our grape arbor, gazing at the golden disc of the
rising full Moon. A chalice for Stonehenge! How should such
a precious thing be made and how wondrous that I would be
chosen to create it. What symbolism would be appropriate?
What was the original purpose of Stonehenge, after all?

Clearly, some honoring of Earth and Heaven. I thought of the interlacing spiral motifs so often used by the people of ancient Britain. The Moon's disc grew more silvery as it rose, its smaller arc echoed by the earth's soft curvature. Two bowls, then. One more shallow, inverted to represent the surface of Mother Earth, and the other suggesting the discs of Sun and Moon. Between them, twining, spiraling elements to serve as a way to hold this chalice, echoing the magical, energetic tie among all three spheres.

The following morning, out in my studio, I rooted through the drawers that held my huge collection of loose gemstones, trays of agates and opals, turquoises and multicolored jaspers, seeking something to represent the polarity of Heaven and Earth. I knew I wanted to use more subtle dome-like cabochon-cut gems rather than glittering, faceted ones. On to the drawer holding the quartz family gems: red and orange carnelian, golden citrine, black onyx, rose quartz, and deep purple amethysts from Siberia and Brazil.

"Which of you want to serve in this special project?" I asked, and in reply, the amethysts and citrines lit up. Purple and gold—how fitting!

I put in a call to the refinery and ordered discs of sterling silver for base and cup and stout round wire from which to forge the twining legs. Over the next two months, I focused on the fabrication of a sterling silver Celtic-inspired cup adorned with gleaming purple amethysts and golden citrines ultimately used in the blessing of those ancient standing stones.

That winter Wellsprings was sold for development, and the local Pagan community lost its sanctuary. Hoping to meet that need, Eric and I worked with others to establish Path of the Moon, a Pagan networking group, which met first at a local park and later at the Winston Salem Unitarian Church. I was eventually elected president of the group, which hosted classes on the Old Ways and monthly full Moon celebrations, along with seasonal celebrations. In addition to tradition and history, we often challenged participants to rethink their framing of reality.

This evening's POTM summer solstice ritual got a bit more intense than I'd anticipated! Tired of attendees complaining about the rituals looking like live-action role play, J. and I decided to pull out all the stops, and he loaned me his great sword for casting the Circle. The event was well attended — close to 40 people — one of the largest groups we've had. About the time we began the ceremony, a big summer storm began to build in the southwest, with ominous black clouds visible through the sanctuary's vaulted windows. Good thing we'd decided to meet indoors!

As usual with this group, folks were restless, and partway into the ritual, one guy heckled, "Show us some real power!"

I've long worked with the weather and it occurred to me to call on the gathering storm. As I hailed mighty Lugh, the Celtic God of the Sun, at the pinnacle of his power in this longest day, I raised the sword toward the heavens and was met by an apocalyptic bolt of lightning striking the church's steeple, blowing the power and leaving us all standing in the dark.

In the back, a shaken voice muttered, "Shit..."

My inner connection with the Divine filled me like a luminous golden river, flowing through my life. My felt connection with the Gods and the spirits around me in nature sang in my blood. Seeing the vast scope of cultural and personal damage wrought by the church, I felt drawn to recover the pre-Christian spiritual legacy of our ancestors and hoped to help others understand the healing I was finding in the Old Ways.

At this point in North Carolina, the great majority of people were (and still are) Christian. Anything having to do with Paganism or the occult was viewed with fear and hostility and equated with the Devil. Determined to do what I could to try to educate the public, I agreed to be interviewed by the local newspapers and appeared as a guest on area television. I was eventually invited to present classes on Paganism and its nature-based spirituality at Western Carolina University, Salem College, and Guilford College.

My presentation at the latter was part of a multidisciplinary program focused on the Moon through the lenses of science, art, and religion. On the night of an autumn full Moon, I spoke to a group of curious and uncertain students. Then, I took them outdoors to the grassy quad where I planned to offer a very simplified Wiccan ceremony. As is often the case when the Moon is full, the sky was filled with clouds. I set up a simple altar and explained the history behind and symbolism of my tools and actions. I invited any students who wished to participate to form a circle with me and suggested that those feeling uncomfortable step back.

About two-thirds of my audience muttered to themselves and gathered in an uneasy group under a large tree. I began my ritual, facing east toward the rising Moon. As I raised my athame, a ceremonial knife intended to direct energy, and pointed toward that heavenly sphere, the clouds conveniently parted to reveal its luminous disc against a starlit sky. I could hear the gasp of astonishment behind me when, just as I finished up my ceremony and opened the circle, the blanket of clouds closed again to conceal the Moon.

Naively, I reasoned that, if the Pagan community were open about what we actually did and debunked the myths, there would be no need to continue to view us as a threat. I failed to appreciate how people will cling to their suppositions, regardless of evidence to the contrary. In my drive to bring local Paganism out of the broom closet, I failed to recognize the blowback my sons were experiencing. These were hard days for them, and they experienced a great deal of prejudice and harassment from their teachers as well as from classmates. Brilliant, understandably angry, and also dealing with learning differences, they floundered in a public school system that had no idea what to do with them.

I finally sued for unpaid child support in order to provide them with help. In response, W. resigned his parental relationship, emancipated his teenage sons, and moved to San Francisco. Although his move didn't solve the child support issue, I felt safe for the first time in many years.

As Path of the Moon grew, there was increased grousing from those attending about the classes and rituals offered. I'd encouraged members to participate in planning and running our events, but received little help. The responsibility of organizing and supporting the group's activities became a burden. Feeling I'd carried the community for long enough, I resigned as the group's president.

My drive for personal authenticity means that I am a "go deep" person, rather than a "go wide" sort. So, I tend to approach whatever I do with intensity and focus. While this is unquestionably rooted in my history of trauma and my autism, it contributes to my need to "get it right." Just as an archaeologist carefully excavates a site, removing layer after layer of concealing soil to expose evidence and indications of past history, I strive to burrow deeper into any interest or belief system, seeking a more authentic understanding.

While I had been active in educating the community about Paganism and creating opportunities for other Earth-spirited folks to come together, I also began to observe a sort of "dumbing down" within the Pagan community as the Old Religion merged with the New Age. No longer interested in the formal instruction available through traditional covens, many self-identified Pagans now seemed simply to be rebellious individuals who rejected the church culture they had been raised in or who were seeking a space in which to explore hedonism. More books on Wicca, magic, and Paganism were appearing, although I found many of them ill-informed. Many of the new converts I met actively rejected the wisdom and guidance of their elders. It seemed to me that I was witnessing a dilution of beliefs, personal discipline, and many of the values I held in high regard. This new Paganism no longer resonated for me. Eric and I once again began to focus on our personal faith journey, rooted in the beliefs and practices of our Celtic and Norse Ancestors — and especially in our relationship with Nature.

Throughout my adult life, I'd lived primarily in cities, in stark contrast to the rich childhood I'd known in the woods of Morrow Mountain. Eric was himself a city kid, having moved to Winston Salem as a toddler, but he had also found sanctuary in the woods near his home. Our term in sacred relationship with the land at Wellsprings made us both aware of a deep and shared longing for a different sort of life than the one we shared in our little suburban brick rancher. We started by looking at Craftsman bungalows in older neighborhoods, drawn to their solidness and proportions. It was quickly apparent that those that had been renovated and updated were beyond our means, and Eric was no handyman.

Then, we visited new homes for sale, only to realize that the McMansions currently in fashion were utterly inconsistent with our values and taste. The Tiny House movement had just begun, and I began to gather books for inspiration, with the thought of actually designing a home for us.

We also began to work magic toward the goal of finding a tract of woods in which we might site such a home. In the Best of All Universes, how might those woods look? How might they feel? I trance-journeyed and was shown old forest bounded by water. Did such a thing even exist in the long-settled Carolina Piedmont? And, if it did, would we even be able to afford it? Increasingly, I felt this land did exist and was waiting for us to find it.

At the same time, on a daily basis, I wondered, *What is real?*

After all, I experienced the world so differently from others, sensing things they do not and dealing with a level of synchronicity well beyond what might be expected through random chance. My therapists and a few trusted friends were encouraging me to start trusting the instincts my well-meaning parents had disabled. As I gradually learned to do so, remarkable things happened.

I was headed out yesterday on my usual round of errands: bank deposit, post office, grocery store, always done in that sequence to take advantage of not having to make left turns across traffic. As I put my key into the ignition, my Higher Guidance said, "Start with the grocery store, then the post office. Go to the bank last."

Why would I feel the need to do that? *I wondered.*

As I pulled out of the driveway, the Voice came again. "Go to the store first."

I actually replied out loud, "That's really inconvenient!"

"Just do it."

And so I did, only to finally arrive at my bank and find it surrounded by police cars and yellow crime scene tape. As it turned out, the bank was being robbed at the very time I would have been there, had I not heeded my intuition.

Eric's ever-present support and encouragement, together with my sons' growing independence, contributed to my success as both artist and spirit-worker. In those days, I thought of myself as a witch and priestess of the Goddess, although my spiritual work was equally rooted in shamanic practice. Most of the self-proclaimed "shamans" I knew of were New Age frauds and pretenders; I felt strongly that I did not want to be grouped with them.

At the same time, I was unaware of any legitimate opportunity for a shamanic apprenticeship related to my own Northern European heritage. Still, I consciously used shamanic techniques, cultivating reciprocity with plant and animal allies, honoring my Ancestors, and using altered states of consciousness to heal people and the land. Having no access to formal shamanic training, I proceeded as I had with my metalwork: I figured out things on my own. Clients learned of me by word of mouth, often engaging me for unusual situations that I had to resolve by instinct.

I got a call yesterday from a woman who's redoing an old farmhouse overlooking the Yadkin. Her workmen keep complaining that something keeps "messing with their equipment," and one of them swore to her that he saw a face looking back at him from the second-story window when no one was up there. She is concerned that they are about to turn tail and run. She wants me to check the place out and, if I find spooks, to deal with them. While most of these calls seem to

be bogus, every so often there's something... there.

(Later) My client's property indeed felt unsettled, and the house itself, built on colonial-era footings, had several rooms on the western side that really felt "off," oppressive, and draining. In a pantry that backed up to what had once been an external root cellar, I could sense that some sort of trauma had occurred. I could barely bring myself to enter and quickly went to work, smudging with a potent mix of dragon's blood and myrrh resins to banish the dark energy and negative presence anchored there. Afterwards, I was able to recommend some steps she could take to improve the flow of energy in the house and others that would help her land to flourish.

I had no shamanic elder to train me and no specific community to serve. I simply found myself thrust, over and over, into situations in which I had to trust my intuition.

However, my intuitive gifts posed their own challenges. For instance, when Eric and I were driving to the coast, we passed a billboard advertising a substantial reward for a missing young woman. "She's dead!" I blurted.

"What? How do you know?" my husband asked, still surprised at times by my Knowing.

"I saw her body in high grass behind a warehouse."

He glanced at me curiously. "Do you have any idea of where?"

"Nope." I'd just glimpsed the flashing image of body, grass, building, and sky. "I mean, even if I knew, how would I go about telling the cops? Their first assumption would be that I was somehow involved."

I stared down at my hands, feeling helpless. "Sometimes this damn Gift is just a burden."

What use was the Knowing of something when I could do nothing? I often confronted this question, such as one morning when I awoke with a great sense of heaviness and mentioned to Eric my intuition that there would be a large earthquake in California. That evening, I learned of the Loma Prieta quake which resulted in the injury of 3,757 and the deaths of 63 persons.

Yet, some of my psychic ability seemed useful. My clairsentience led me to the book store for just the right book, told me who was calling before I ever answered the phone, and often cued me where to find various items. It also alerted me to illness in others.

That fall, my mother happened to mention a knot at the base of her neck near her collarbone. "I think it's probably just a swollen lymph gland, nothing to worry about," she insisted. She'd been depressed and often tired, so I was concerned.

I asked her if I could explore it. The mass I found on closer examination alarmed me. "I really think you should have your doctor check it. Better to know, don't you think?" The subsequent biopsy indicated poorly-differentiated carcinoma, cancer, and a grave prognosis.

As she always had, she minimized her fears and kept a brave face. "You have a life to live, and I want you to live it," she said. "I don't always understand why you do the things you do or why you make everything so complicated. You've had a rough go of things, but I can see that you and Eric are happy together, and I want you to cherish this time. Look for the land you talk about, build that home you dream of, and I'll help as best I can."

Season Three

Summer, Ripening

The heavy quilt of August
Drapes cornfields and sweltering orchards
As thunderheads tower, building.
Far to the west, the deep cadence of thunder
Bespeaks the storm to come.
Tall cornstalks march in martial rows
While swollen squash and sweet melons
Ripen in the heat.
Murmuring in contentment, the bees beard their hives,
Redolent of honey and smoke.
I soak away my aches in a stream warm as a bathtub.
Above me, on a birch bough,
A lone kingfisher preens his emerald breast,
Then drops to spear a frog.
I will arise from these sun-touched waters,
With hope renewed, and make my quiet way
To where the deer graze,
gazing at me with enquiring eyes.
I am learning the ways and rhythms of this land
 as I am learning myself.
Through purple twilight's gloaming I walk homeward,
My passage lit by dancing fireflies.
Oh, that I am privileged to such mysteries.

Eight
SANCTUARY

The search for a parcel of forested land for our home-to-be became the focus of our free time, driving back roads on Sunday
afternoons, looking and feeling for the right place. We poured
a tremendous amount of care and intention into a wish list
describing the qualities our perfect tract would have: mature
trees, a body of water, and a sense of lively spirit. Thanks to
generous bequests from my aunts and uncle, we were able to
build up a nest egg and eventually engaged a broker to help
us in our search.

On one frosty afternoon in late January of 2001, I asked her
to show me land near the tiny hamlet of Germanton, just north
of Winston Salem. Once home to the Indigenous Saura people,
by the mid-1700s, German emigrants had settled the village
that was named for them, drawn to the region's plentiful game
and rich, fertile soil. The area was rural, filled with sweetly
rolling farmland and steeply forested ridges. It was also close
enough to Winston Salem for Eric to easily commute.

"The property out there is mostly held by a few old families and doesn't turn over often," the broker advised, taking
a moment to think. "There was a parcel on the market for
awhile, but when the county was talking about damming
Town Fork Creek, the owners took it off. I have no idea of the
status, but we can still check it out."

At my urging, she drove us through rugged foothills into
a broad valley where horses grazed and cornstalks marked
well-tended croplands. We turned off and rumbled across an
old steel truss bridge over a stream, emerging into something
magical. The land on the other side felt like nothing else we'd
seen, sweet and loved, and reminded me immediately of the

Uwharrie Mountains where I'd grown up. Our broker parked and I popped out of her car to follow a well-worn trail along Town Fork Creek.

My sense of wonder rose along with the stark, towering cliffs cut by that watercourse and adorned with glittering ice-daggers. Along the stream, huge poplar and river birch trees towered like the columns of a temple. The bluff above was draped with mounds of tangled mountain laurel and glossy rhododendron, while evergreen hemlocks offered a soft, blue-green buffer from the modern world. I clambered up the steep hillside to emerge into a slight clearing, the broker puffing and struggling behind me. A neighbor was able to point out the boundary markers and told us that the area had once been part of a large family farm that was divided into lots for development in the 1960s. At my request, our broker promised she'd research the property.

That evening, when Eric came in from work, I informed him that I was going to pack a picnic lunch and pick him up from work the following day to show him "our land." He responded as strongly as I did, and we began to figure how we might purchase the property, which proved to be two pie-shaped lots owned by a pair of brothers. Much of the land had been cropland, now forested floodplain, and while a treasure-trove of Nature, unsuitable for building. To have access to the road and enough room to build on the bluff, we realized we would need to purchase both parcels, a total of over 12 acres. We negotiated with the brothers, eventually settling on an exceptionally fair price. With my mother's blessings, we closed on the land in May.

Our sons, now fine young men, had embarked upon independent lives. One moved to California to study film makeup and special effects, and, later, his brother moved to Asheville to attend technical college. It was a time of much chaos in the family of my birth: my successful younger brother's alcohol-ism had caught up with him, costing him his six-figure job and his marriage. He often called up drunk and maudlin, bounc-ing in and out of treatment centers. My father continued to be his usual volatile and often irrational self, even as my mother was undergoing radiation treatment for her cancer and trying to rescue my brother. While Mom was excited for us as we made plans for a new life, my father was resentful that we had no interest in taking over the mountain homestead he'd come to love.

Eric and I spent all our free time exploring our woods. Several evenings a week, we'd drive up from town, often bringing sausages to grill on sticks over the small firepit the prior owners had made on the top of the bluff. We sat by the fire, listening to the wind, the owls, and the whippoorwills calling mournfully in the wet bottomland near the stream. We courted the spirit of the property, leaving offerings, inviting the land and its various biomes and residents to reveal them-selves.

Our explorations showed us that we'd purchased an ex-ceptional tract of land. Perhaps due to the microclimate cre-ated by the stream and surrounding Saura Hills, the plants and trees were atypical for the Carolina Piedmont, more like those one might find at around 4,000 feet in the Blue Ridge mountains. We found we were home to numerous rare native plants, edible and medicinal. Deer and foxes, weasels, opos-sums, raccoons, and even a bear roamed the forest. The vari-ety of bird life was impressive, as was the diversity of reptiles and amphibians.

We found where wagon ruts carved the face of the bluff and where rusting remnants of the barbed wire that had enclosed cattle spanned from tree to tree around the hillside. The silty bottomland still bore the undulations of the farmer's plough. A chevron of stones across the stream marked where the native Saura people had once maintained a fish weir. People long prior to us had left their mark on this land — how would we engage with it? We wanted this venture to be a partnership, collaborating with Nature rather than exploiting Her.

A few weeks ago, as Eric and I were exploring the land, I came across a young, lightning-struck cedar tree. Something about it spoke to me and, as Thor's bolt had already killed it, I got Eric to cut it down. After I'd gotten it home, I realized that earlier in its short life, it had been entwined by honeysuckle and thus forced into a spiraling form perfect for a magical staff.

Somehow, it seemed important to avoid using steel tools on it. So, instead, I used sharp obsidian flakes to scrape away the papery bark. Once cleaned, it was evident that the staff terminated in one small lateral branch and a serpent's head! I continued to scrape and polish, attaching a small antler to the branch with a bronze collar and rivets. I mounted a deep red carnelian as the serpent's eye and whimsically added a red leather tongue. Something compelled me to add the runes to the staff, so I placed them intuitively, carving them into the rosy fragrant wood, then waxed the staff to a fine sheen. What a powerful tool, resonant with fire and earth!

A huge part of the delight of owning land was the process of discovery and establishing friendships with the other Beings who shared it. Close by the small clearing that surrounded our little fire pit were a pair of beech trees, each perhaps thirty years old. I have loved beeches since my childhood for their smooth, silvery bark and finely serrated leaves that turn a rich tan in autumn, clinging throughout the winter to warm the dreary landscape. As a child, I was convinced that they were the magical golden Mallorn trees that J. R. R. Tolkien described in his books, *The Hobbit* and *The Lord of the Rings* series.

During our frequent visits to our land, we were observant, noting where the Sun and Moon rose and set through the course of the seasons. We found that the storms tended to move in from the southwest and that our land was sheltered by a high ridge that diverted those storms. As I contemplated a plan for the small passive-solar cottage we hoped to build, I asked the land to show me how best to situate the structure. Toward our eastern boundary, high on the bluff above the stream, a spot revealed itself: the location of our firepit. The beeches that stood to the southeast and west would offer cooling shade in the summer. Their winter leaves could act as a windbreak and offer color in an otherwise drab season. I came to view them as dear friends. When, in time, we began the construction of our little cottage, I made sure to erect conspicuous fencing to ensure our beeches would be safe from clumsy workmen and backhoes.

The beech to the southeast of the house site anchors a natural area filled with bluebells, ferns, and trout lilies. Its pale gray, mottled trunk is almost two feet in diameter at the base. In summer, the long undulating branches cast deep shade that will shelter our cottage from the Sun's heat.

To the west, another will embrace our elevated deck and bedroom, blessing us with the sense that we are living in a tree house. All through the winter, her silvery, twining boughs are dressed in glossy tan leaves that sizzle in snow and sleet, or rattle and whisper in the wind. The descending sun sets them alight and they glow a rich gold. As the land gradually warms in spring, she awakens from her winter slumber, and sweet sap begins to rise within her. Then, on a warm and windy day in late spring, a day chosen by some arcane biological magic, she lets go her tawny cloak, and the leaves that have adorned her throughout the winter whirl free, borne by the wind to add their nutrients to the forest duff.

Over the following week, her leaf buds swell within shiny tan husks until their growing bulk splits the casings, and tender, lime-green spirals of new foliage unwind and spread. Within four or five days, the bare twigs are laden with fresh new leaves. Among the gnarled gray roots, mossy earth below is once again shaded and cool. I will watch this process from my bedroom window: tan wintery leaves setting sail, swelling new growth, and finally, rich green foliage casting sweet dappled shade across my bed.

Grandmother Beech, I thank you for the gift of beauty in all seasons. You teach me that Nature is not static and that all things change, even as I now watch your swelling buds and await the unfurling of your fresh chartreuse gown. Where ice has broken limbs, you've adapted and put out lateral branches. Where a surveyor long ago marked a boundary with a metal stake, your strong, white wood gradually teaches me that boundaries are manmade and transient. You honor your own inner wisdom, not bound to any human calendar.

My mother's health continued to decline, and she was hospitalized in early March of 2002 near death. She slowly recovered enough to be able to come home for a few weeks, and I had my final visit with her at the end of April. Two weeks later, she phoned to ask me to stay with her until her passing, but died early the next morning before I could reach her.

I spent the rest of the week with my father, who was as irrational and abusive with me as he had been with my mother. Feeling responsible for him, as I always somehow had, I did my best to comfort and support him. In his pain, he struck out verbally.

"He needs you," some family members urged.

"He'll destroy you," others warned.

Ultimately, his persistent cruelty left me no choice but to distance myself out of self-preservation, one of the hardest decisions I've ever faced.

The rest of the year was a fog of grief. Often awakening at 3 a.m., I would get up and work on sketches for the little house we longed to build, inspired by the Craftsman style we both loved. I was determined to keep the project as small and "green" as possible. I began to experience lucid dreams in which I visited some alternate reality where the house already existed to wander around inside, making mental notes — only to awaken and modify the plans I was working on, shifting window placement and room dimensions to conform to the dream house. In a very real sense, I dreamed our cottage into being.

We interviewed potential builders, seeking someone who felt compatible with our values and who would approach the land with respect. The banks proved unwilling to finance the small, non-traditional home we wanted to build, although they were more than willing to underwrite a huge brick monstrosity. Finally, an acquaintance suggested that we contact the Farm Credit Bureau, who proved both open minded and very creative.

"Do you have any flat land?" the friendly agent asked.

Eric and I looked at one another uncertainly. "Uh, yes. About six acres used to be cultivated."

"Great! We'll designate you as a hay farm."

"But that land is all covered with trees now!" I blurted.

"OK. But you *could* clear and farm it, right?" He winked, inviting us into the conspiracy. "That lets us consider this an agricultural loan. Then, it doesn't matter if you want to build a cottage or a silo."

I found a drafting student from the local technical college to convert my drawings into proper blueprints for our small, passive solar Craftsman cottage. Ultimately we engaged a builder, and the loan was approved using our land as collateral. We carefully and prayerfully cleared our home site as the spirits of the property had instructed me.

Neighbors indicated that the water table was problematic. Their wells produced iron-rich, sulfur-reeking water, occasionally running dry in late summer. In the hope that we might manage to find a better water source, I hired the most highly recommended professional dowser in the southeast to pinpoint where we needed to drill, only to have the county engineer subsequently inform us that our planned well site was 50 feet too close to where the septic system was to go. The drilling truck was already scheduled for the following Monday, which left no time to bring the dowser back.

I could dowse, but did I trust my skill? A lot was on the line.

Eric and I drove out the following morning, and I said a prayer to the land spirits, asking them to guide me to the best place for us to drill for good water. Unlike the pro we'd hired, who used the traditional y-shaped branch as a dowsing tool, I rely on how my body senses underground water. Some 60 feet further west from the original site, I located what was clearly a blind spring (one which doesn't reach the surface) where deep pressure brings water up beneath an impervious stone cap. My Knowing told me that we would hit water at 260 feet and that the well would yield over 10 gallons a minute. This was unheard of in our neighborhood, where many wells were 800 feet deep and produced only 3 or 4 gallons a minute. Still, all we could do was to mark the spot with a flag and carefully release the spirits of the trees we had to clear to make way for the drilling rig.

On Monday morning while Eric was at work, I watched anxiously as the well drilling truck slogged across our muddy building site and into place over our orange flag. I settled myself against a huge old hemlock whose fallen needles offered a thick cushion and began to sing to the underground water, a chant of thanks and delight.

Hour after hour, the drill bored into Mother's breast, each added pipe marking ten more feet. I could feel the vibrations and prayed I'd been right. At 2:30 p.m. in the afternoon, the drill suddenly dropped and water began to jet from the casings. The driller measured the flow: 12 gallons a minute at 263 feet; no iron; no sulfur.

Some weeks later, in a local gallery and gift shop, I came across a pale green Arts and Crafts tile carved with the image of a pair of trees supporting each other. The image seemed the perfect metaphor for the relationship Eric and I shared, and it offered inspiration for the hand-made tiles that would surround our fireplace as well as a magnificent stained glass window that now hangs in our great room.

On the day that the footings were poured, I sprinkled my mother's ashes at each corner of the house, honoring her as my foundation. Construction proceeded smoothly, and, with each passing day, we saw my drawings become a home. Just after Thanksgiving of 2004, on a cold, sleety day, we moved into the shingle-sided cottage we'd named TwoTrees.

Life continued to be a roller-coaster. In January of 2005, just after we celebrated closing on our new home, Eric lost his job. We battened down the hatches in an effort to get by and got creative with beans and rice. As quickly as possible, we readied our old house in town for sale, accepting a low-ball offer so we wouldn't have to carry two mortgages.

The therapy I'd experienced had primarily focused on my depression, but equally problematic was my anxiety, the overwhelming fear that I would do something wrong or was wrong myself. Having learned from my mother to use food for self-comfort, I also used it to manage the anxiety of being radically different: deeply intuitive, in a body that often felt alien and overwhelmed by hypersensitivity. Although no one had actually used the term "eating disorder" with me, I understood that my use of food was unhealthy and taking a toll on my body.

Knowing that my brother was struggling with recovery and perhaps struggling himself, my father offered to give Reid his big old two-story farmhouse, provided my brother would help care for him. Pop planned to build a small house better suited to his needs. Given my issues with my dad, this initially seemed like an arrangement beneficial to all parties. Reid agreed and moved down from Pennsylvania, unexpectedly bringing with him a woman he'd befriended in rehab, whom he would soon marry. She proved an adept manipulator and quickly convinced my father to build the new house for them, instead.

I began to feel concerned over the arrangement. Pop's erratic behavior and compulsive spending increased. His driving was terrifying. He was eventually diagnosed with hydro-cephalus and early Alzheimer's disease. After having a shunt implanted to reduce his intracranial pressure, Pop recovered quickly and experienced a profound change in personality, becoming very sweet and loving. The change was remarkable, leaving me to wonder how long the hydrocephalus had been a factor in his belligerence.

On one occasion, when we'd brought Pop down for a medical checkup with his neurologist, we had him stay overnight with us, his first visit to TwoTrees.

"Is this a park?" he asked, confused.

"No Daddy. This is Eric's and my home near Winston Salem."

He gazed around, trying to make sense of the unfamiliar. "This is a nice house. How did you find it?"

I smiled. "I designed it, and we had someone build it for us."

"Well, y'all did a bang-up job! I had no idea you knew how to build a house."

During this time, my brother and new sister-in-law managed to obtain my father's Power-of-Attorney and began to systematically exclude me from all decisions involving his care. Following a small fire at Pop's house caused by an electrical short in his well pump, they removed everything of value and tossed the remainder of my parents' things into boxes stuffed into several rooms while repairs were undertaken. Selling the new home my father had built for them, they abruptly moved to Greensboro and placed him in a nearby assisted living facility.

In contrast with our previously strained relationship, this was a surprisingly sweet time for me with my dad. Taking breaks from my work at the jeweler's bench or with shamanic clients, I visited him often — taking him to lunch, singing old songs with him as I cut his hair, and doing what I could to assure him that I loved him. He no longer remembered all the hurtful things he had once said and done, and he often spoke wistfully of his parents and childhood.

During this time, I received major commissions from the University of Mary Washington and Emory and Henry College to design and create major pieces of ceremonial regalia for them. Our financial situation began to improve. At the same time, the years of stress and trauma had taken their toll on my health. Diagnosed with diabetes and high blood pressure, I was encouraged by my endocrinologist to consider a gastric bypass to help me lose weight, but our health insurance wouldn't cover the surgery because it was then considered experimental.

The following spring, we were stunned when my brother and sister-in-law announced that they were moving to Kansas City to be near her family — and that they were taking Pop with them. They informed us that we were to pack and ship his possessions and, then, to escort my bewildered father by air to Missouri. That bitter February, it fell to Eric and me to sort through the jumbled boxes in an empty, frigid house lacking power or running water, preparing my parents' remaining belongings for an auction to generate funds for his care. I gritted my teeth, packed and labeled, and told myself I was doing it for my father.

The following year, changes in Eric's health insurance finally made it possible for me to undergo weight-loss surgery. I began the meetings, tests, and evaluations that prepared me for the procedure. I had tried to address my eating disorder in every way I knew and was aware that it was slowly killing me. My CAH, an endocrine condition, was an underlying factor, but years of unhealed trauma also played a major role. I knew that I used food for comfort and, more significantly, to manage anxiety. My bulk also helped to filter the overwhelming incoming stimuli from the worlds and the many Beings around me. Knowing things can go wrong during major surgery, I was frightened, but believed this was my best option for better health.

In December of 2007, on my 55th birthday, I finally underwent gastric bypass surgery, recovering enough by Yule to climb part way up Pilot Mountain for our annual solstice rite. This life-saving surgery, along with determination and significant life changes, made it possible for me to eventually lose a total of 180 pounds; while I still wasn't thin, I felt comfortable in my body for the first time in my life, my high blood pressure resolved, and my diabetes was cured. While I realize that this radical solution doesn't work for everyone, I have no doubt that it saved my life by helping shift my habits and coping mechanisms.

By this time, my brother and his wife had moved my dad to a V.A. facility in Cameron, Missouri, where, several months into his residence, he fell and broke his hip. Although surgery went well, Pop continued to deteriorate. I awakened one morning with the strong premonition that my father was dying. Eric and I got the first tickets we could find and flew out for a final precious visit with him, parting in peace. He crossed four days later.

When I eventually received my copy of his will, the contents proved quite disturbing. My attorney and a forensic accountant confirmed malfeasance, but circumstances made it impractical to pursue legal recourse. I felt sad and furious and impotent.

Perhaps in response to the profound frustration I felt, I poured myself into a deeper relationship with our property. My weight loss left me with lots more energy, and I was able to truly enjoy gardening and woods work for the first time in my life. The hilltop where we'd built had poor, thin topsoil, so we built a group of raised beds that I filled with vegetables and healing herbs and perennials. Rather than a tidy lawn, we planted the area cleared for our septic field with a wildflower meadow.

Just as Eric and I had asked the spirits of our land to instruct us in how we could build our home to respect and compliment the natural environment, we also asked to be guided to locations where we could create spaces for worship. One of the first and most obvious was a spot at the base of the creekside cliffs. There, long ago, a huge wedge of stone had split from the bluff to land as a bulwark to the stream, creating a small, chapel-like space, which was still and private. The location suggested a stone altar, and a spring flood gifted us with a slab of sandstone the size of a bench top. We made offerings of cornmeal and tobacco to the spirit of the place and placed the slab on a pair of large terra cotta chimney flues that raised it to waist height.

The process of drilling our well had left us with a small clearing over the quartzite dome downhill from the house, and the upwelling energy there made it the perfect complement to the space near the cliffs. In the spirit of ancient megalithic structures like Stonehenge, we decided to build a stone circle. The following summer, Eric and I negotiated with rocks in the stream, seeking those that might be willing to be part of a stone circle. Roughly a dozen offered themselves. Once we had muscled them out of the creek, up the bank and into the back of my Nissan Murano, we drove them up the hill to the house and transferred them into the wheelbarrow. Down the hill at the site, we grabbed a compass and marked the four directions. The largest stone and several willing supporters were situated in the north to serve as the altar, leaving three other large stones as uprights and three smaller ones to be placed at their bases. We shuffled stones and listened in until the stones and the site all seemed content. We felt quite pleased with how the structure amplified the heavenward thrust of earth energy.

On the next full moon, we began a month-long cycle of consecrating the space to the Norse brother and sister deities Freyr and Freyja, whom we'd begun to honor. Considered by the Norse to be members of a race of Gods known as the Vanir, we associated these sacred twins with fertility and harvest.

When insect damage forced us to take down several large loblolly pines, we cut them into stout drums and arranged them around the perimeter of the circle, transplanting willing ferns from the surrounding woods to soften the effect. In the East, the direction of Air, we hung a wind chime I had made in the form of a dragonfly. From thin copper sheet, I formed a whirl of dancing flames for the South, direction of Fire and of creativity. In the West, the direction of Water, we placed a large abalone shell, with its iridescent blues and purples a reminder of the flow of emotions. Beneath the altar, we set a large cluster of clear quartz crystals as a reminder of Earth, grounding and manifestation. The whole space was lit by four large iron torchieres and connected with the lower altar via the winding path created by our deer. In some intangible way, the upper *Ve*, a Norse term for a sacred space, became the beating ceremonial heart of TwoTrees, a place where we made love, left offerings, mourned, and celebrated.

As the land changed, so did the landscape of my body, once encased by over 350 pounds of armor and pain. Additional surgeries were necessary to remove the folds of redundant skin so that I could move more freely and comfortably, and I began to understand just how much I had used my bulk to buffer the psychic noise of the world around me. It was a blessing that I no longer lived in the city.

During this time, I actively honed my skills at divination. Just as my maternal grandmother read people's fortunes in tea leaves and playing cards, I had learned to use tarot cards and, then, the runes. From the dawn of time and in cultures around the world, people have sought insight and guidance through this sacred art. The term "divination" means utilizing a system of signs or symbols in combination with a mildly altered state of consciousness with the intention of accessing information and guidance otherwise not readily available. Divination may be done for one's own benefit or in service to a client. While there are specific considerations in the latter circumstances, the foundation of the practice is the same for both circumstances.

Divination connects us with culture and history and with the many thousands of diviners before us. Secondly, it connects us with the information embedded within Universal Causality. New Age practitioners often refer to the Akashic records. A Greek *Mantis* might reference *Moirai* (the Fates), or a Yoruba *Babalawo* the *Odu Ifa*, while the Norse speak of the *Wyrd*, the vast web of causality spun, woven, and cut by the three sisters known as Norns. There are many active agents or players in this web of causality. From an animistic point of view, all objects have spirits or personhood that influence the world around them.

We gather information through education and research and our personal experiences, using the commonly acknowledged five senses. However, we also gather information through prayer and meditation or intuition and psychic gifts. Intuitive ability is like any other talent: Some individuals are innately blessed with intuitive ability, but others must work diligently to develop it. Like painting or playing the piano, concentration and regular practice strengthen one's skills.

Divinatory techniques vary widely, from *Shagai*, the Mongolian art of throwing sheep knucklebones, to tarot cards and Norse runes. All use some combination of tools, symbols, skills, and the intuitive gifts of the Diviner. Divination as a process is one of our earliest spiritual practices and was initially tied to our relationship with the natural world and desire to survive. Imagine living in a time when knowing where the caribou migration will cross the river is the difference between adequate food for the winter or starvation. Divination systems may be traditional (in which specific meanings are assigned to particular symbols or combination of signs) or self-created (in which the diviner assigns his or her own meaning to given symbols or creates his or her own symbolic layout).

Historically, diviners have served their communities as either shamans or as priests, held in high regard. With the coming of Christianity, divination came to be regarded as evil. In many places it is still illegal; it is still disparaged by being referred to as "fortune telling." However, divination offered a helpful means of harnessing my gifts—one I used for clients and for myself.

By this point in time, many aspects of my life had shifted. My children were grown. My parents were both dead, and now I was alienated from my brother. I was still learning how to manage my new life in a body much changed by my surgeries. Most importantly, my spiritual beliefs and practices had evolved in ways that had me often looking to divination for insight and guidance—and that divination told me that a major change was coming.

 *Ten*

Silver had been a theme flowing through my life, even before my long, dark hair began to gray. While I also worked with gold, my preferred metal of choice had always been silver: luminous, receptive, and capable of being shaped, formed, and textured in so many ways, ever offering itself as the physical metaphor of Light and Shadow. As I healed from my gastric bypass surgery and my brother's betrayal, silver entered my life in a new and unexpected way.

All of my life, I have loved and enjoyed cats and found them beautiful, amusing, and comforting. One day, while writing at my computer, I decided to take a break and casually followed a link to an animal rescue site. Among the many available cats, one small triangular face caught my eye, and I saw something special. When I showed Eric the photo, he knew I'd been hooked.

That Saturday, we visited the shelter. Their cat room was filled with dozens of felines of all colors and sizes. Yet, when I sat down on the floor, that particular tiny gray fluff ball made a beeline across the room to clamber into my lap where he rolled onto his back and gazed adoringly into my eyes. He was a long-haired Russian Blue or Nebelung and has matured into a huge, silky, silver lion of exceptional sensitivity.

Among all the many cats who have shared my life, Tristan remains the most special, a natural healer who is exceptionally aware of my emotional state. During my recoveries from the numerous illnesses and surgeries I have undergone, he situates himself on my chest, heart-to-heart, and gazes lovingly at me through wise, half-closed, peridot eyes. As I type this, he lies on the table beside me, one huge paw tenderly resting on my hand, his deep purr filling the room.

My explorations of shamanism and work as a metalsmith continued to be entwined in uncanny ways that were to impress upon me the weight of my calling. Clearly, the jewelry I created was something more to my clients. Couples sought me out to create their wedding rings, desiring the deeply personal magic and symbolism I brought to the process. Customers brought heirlooms, asking me to design and create talismans honoring deceased loved ones. Protective jewelry I created was carried into war zones and worn into hostile business meetings. I made cradle charms for newborns and crosses for newly ordained ministers and Torah pointers given as memorial gifts to synagogues.

The sunny studio building, which had been our first construction at TwoTrees, faced northward, the 12-by-16-foot building raised on stout timbers at the edge of the bluff. Its shed roof, pierced with skylights, vaulted toward a series of big windows framing a view of the hemlocks and old-growth beeches overlooking Town Fork Creek. This was my sanctuary, with areas for design and fabrication, storage for precious metals and my large collection of gems and beads, the bench where I fabricated my work, and a polishing area. The walls were hung with artwork and jewelry design sketches, deer antlers, and an altar with treasures from the land. Another small altar overlooked my soldering table, dedicated to the smithing Gods of various cultures: Celtic Brighid, Germanic Volund, Greek Hephaestus and the Norse Dwarves or Duergar. Stepping into that studio was, for me, like entering a church. I queued up music that I loved, greeted the Holy Powers, and dropped into the altered state in which I birthed the inspired and enchanted objects that flowed from my hands; this was a state wherein whether I was male or female or both was irrelevant.

Throughout this time, I worked instinctively, developing my shamanic and artistic skills with no formal instruction or guidance. I hungered for deeper training, yet knew of no relevant resources. Such had been the pattern all my life: that I learned by doing and struggled to find my way in a life unlike that of anyone else I knew. My lessons continued to come in the form of dreams and visions, often when I was sick, forming connections with spirit teachers long before I recognized them. As often happens with individuals who have undergone gastric bypass surgery, I developed gallstones, becoming critically ill when they blocked a duct. In the throes of a raging fever, I journeyed afar.

I am trudging through a blizzard in high craggy mountains, and twilight clouds give everything a luminous blue glow. I know that it is imperative for me to find shelter or I will die of exposure. As I look out across a wide valley, I can see a glowing cave, almost like a mouth, high up on a peak across the way. There is clearly a fire inside, and I must somehow get to that cave. When I finally reach the entrance, long drips of ice hang down like sharp teeth; I am afraid to pass under them and go within.

Inside, the cave rises in a high vault and is illuminated by the dancing light of a number of fires. On the stone floor of the cave is carved a labyrinth: this is clearly a Holy Place. I am greeted by four elder priestesses, robed in black, who will watch over me. They undress me and rub my naked body with red ocher.

One of the crones offers me a bowl of dried Amanita mushrooms; I choose and consume three. Once I have eaten them, I am made to lie down on a bearskin at the center of the labyrinth and told I am to "Go within the belly of the Mother." The crones arrange me on my left side, in a fetal position, like a body for a burial. They scatter over my body anemone petals and tiny white beads ground from shells. I wonder where they found the purple and white flowers in the midst of winter.

One begins to drum, while the others begin to sing in an eerie ancient keening tongue. The flames cast leaping shadows against the cave walls, and it feels like there are many people gathered expectantly in the darkness around us. As the mushrooms take effect, I slip away into blackness.

That summer, I was contacted by the woman I'd worked for at Wellsprings, who had relocated to the affluent vacation town of Blowing Rock, where she owned a realty company specializing in the up-scale properties of that mountain resort. Her office featured a gallery area, and I was invited to display my jewelry as part of a two-person exhibition, a remarkable opportunity, given the wealth of that artsy community. I doubled down, creating a body of almost seventy-five new pieces, and Eric and I packed up my jewelry and displays and headed west.

We have been invited to stay at L.'s dramatic mountain-top home, a museum-like space filled with masks, carvings, and other sacred objects gathered by her on her many trips abroad. Making us welcome, she led us to a guest room filled with brightly painted folk art, baskets, and tapestries from Mexico and Guatemala. Hallway niches held sacred carvings from Nigeria and Cameroon, and a four-hundred-year-old Burmese statue of the Buddha towered over the living room.

After the long day and an elaborate dinner, we were exhausted, falling into bed. Eric slept soundly, while I tossed and turned. The long night brought a procession of anguished spirits from sacred objects relegated to the role of décor. They stood at the bedside, knowing I could hear and see them, pleading for offerings, for recognition, for repatriation to the lands from which they were taken. As I walked through the house on my way to breakfast the following morning, they reached out to me again, pleading for the devotion and care they had previously received.

One of the important roles a shaman plays is that of intercessor between consensual reality and the realms of the Spirits, and, in that capacity, I felt compelled to try to help my hostess understand that her inanimate art objects were, in fact, enspirited and desperately hungry for celebration and respect. The stewardship of such Sacred Things requires care and devotion. As we drove the short distance to the gallery, I told her about my experience and spoke eloquently of the importance of recognizing the responsibility that accompanies ownership of Sacred Objects.

To my horror, she laughed brashly and said that it was a good thing that she wasn't a shaman so she wouldn't have to put up with all those spirits visiting her.

As soon as the exhibition was over, we quickly packed my work and, with heavy hearts and a deep sense of wrongness, came home.

Having broken away from the local Pagan community ten years previously and spiritually focused in our sacred relationship with TwoTrees, Eric and I increasingly thought of ourselves as Heathen and honored the Gods of our Norse ancestors. While Heathenism can be loosely placed under the wider Pagan umbrella and shares certain beliefs in common with Paganism, many of the beliefs and practices are more directly informed by ancestral Northern European spirituality.

Because we have no information on Norse spiritual practices recorded by the culture itself prior to forced conversion, modern worshipers of the Norse Gods base their practices on reconstructions based in the archaeological evidence, texts recorded after the Viking Era, and personal gnosis. Individuals who identify as Heathen are likely to look specifically to the sacred practices of ancient Germanic and Scandinavian people. Like contemporary Christianity, modern Heathenism encompasses a wide range of variants ranging from very conservative, oath-based groups to those that are inclusive and diverse — values much in keeping with the practices of their Ancestors.

The diversity of Norse culture was reflected in their animistic and polytheistic spiritual beliefs and practices. An individual's relationship with the Sacred appears to have been a highly personal matter, with rites and practices varying from person to person and farmstead to farmstead. There was no central religious authority, no holy book, few temples, and the scattered clergy appear to have been dedicated to the service of particular deities and the offerings made to those deities. Magic and spirituality were deeply intertwined, underpinned by a deep reverence for the Dead, and society was bound by sworn oaths and the concepts of courage, honor, and obligation.

Since most self-identified Heathens were raised Christian and later converted, they tend to bring with them certain expectations inconsistent with what we know of historical Norse religion: a central holy book to offer spiritual guidance, an expectation that clergy will mitigate between them and the Gods, and a misguided sense of orthodoxy. Certain core precepts of Heathen belief, such as sacred exchange and reciprocity, honor, and loyalty, have little sway in the twenty-first century, meaning that modern Heathens must actively struggle to unlearn certain Christian and Western beliefs and replace them with others more authentic — or else warp the spiritual heritage of the religion.

The public picture of modern Heathenism has also been fouled by neo-Nazi groups that have appropriated our Gods and sacred symbols, much to the dismay of the greater Heathen community — and the confusion of the general public. In contrast to the racist and xenophobic agendas promoted by these problematic groups, historical Norse culture benefitted from trading contacts and interactions with other cultures as far afield as Central Asia, the Mediterranean, and North Africa. DNA studies of Norse remains indicate a surprising amount of intermarriage. Being a particularly pragmatic culture, the Norse were quick to adopt skills, beliefs, and practices from other cultures that they found useful. Archaeologist Neil Price, distinguished professor and chair of archaeology at Uppsala University, Sweden, has drawn strong conclusions regarding the adoption of Sámi shamanic practices by the Norse, especially in the practice of *seidr* or magic.

In the fall of 2012, I began to experience an eerie sense of being "stalked" by a Presence I eventually identified as the one-eyed shaman God and rune bringer, first worshiped by the ancient horse people migrating westward from the steppe, and later known as Wotan or Odin. I had read enough about Him to be wary of engaging, knowing that He often exacted a high price for any help He offered and that He was known to occasionally drive those who served Him mad.

Walking in the river forest of TwoTrees, with its curious, folded energy, I felt His presence: grave, wondrous, and terrifying. Fearing I might inadvertently invoke Him, I would only refer to Him using the *heiti* or by-names which referenced His many aspects: All-Father, Wanderer, High One, Frenzy.

Frenzy—that word which is also the meaning of the root word for shaman.

Recently, just before I drop into a deep sleep, I've begun experiencing the most remarkable lucid dreams! They open with my following a trail through our forested bottom land, my staff in hand, and my beloved spirit cat Tristan at my side. In the dreams, Tristan is huge, the size of a collie.

The winding trail leads to a screen of white birch saplings, and, beyond, I can see a shallow frozen pond at the foot of a huge tree. Vague white shapes float beneath the ice. In each dream, I approach the pond, ask a question, shatter the ice with my staff, and runes rise to the surface to offer guidance. It's notable that, in Norse mythology, ice is one of the primordial elements of creation, and Yggdrasil, the World Tree, is rooted in the Well of Urd, the source of the wisdom associated with the runes.

Ultimately, these dreams culminate with an encounter with Odin, lounging at the foot of the tree, smoking His pipe, and looking a great deal like Tolkien's Gandalf—not surprisingly, as the writer intentionally based the character on descriptions of the All-Father from Norse and Anglo-Saxon lore.

Well before the production of the television drama *Vikings* spawned a flood of interest in All Things Norse, the North called, and, with it, my life began to come full circle. I learned to use the images from my dreams as an active divination process, visualizing myself walking to the rune pool, asking a question, stirring the waters with my staff, and taking note of the runes that floated to the surface. I have studied and worked with these magical symbols for many years; Eric's and my wedding rings bore inscriptions in runes and a panel carved with protective bindrunes guarded our front door. My husband grew out his chestnut beard, and I eventually started braiding it in two plaits for him, each clasped with silver spirals. Both of us worked with a local tattoo artist who understood the depth of our beliefs and who ceremonially inked sacred designs on our bodies.

Beginning that spring, we hosted several seasonal *sumbels* – Heathen rituals of toasting and praise in which I served as *Gythja* or priest – attended by a handful of friends. Our connection with the spiritual traditions of the North grew deeper as our life centered on our relationship with our land and the many Beings sharing it with us.

Interacting with the Goddess Freyja and her twin brother Freyr caused me to reflect on how I am a vessel for Both. I'd encountered references to the importance that non-traditionally gendered individuals play as healers and spiritual advisors in many cultures. Native Americans view gender differently from tribe to tribe, and, among the Indigenous people of Siberia and Mongolia, it is common for practitioners of shamanism to transgress Western gender norms. In many cases, these individuals were understood to possess particular gifts, insights, and powers. Exploring this crosscultural pattern offered welcome perspective. I finally realized that being both masculine and feminine made it easier for me to stand simultaneously in both consensual reality and the spirit realms.

Eric and I had long honored these Sacred Twins as deities of fertility, agriculture, and animal husbandry. Many bits of Germanic and Scandinavian lore refer to the Vanic siblings who were sent as peace hostages to the realms of the Aesir following a long and terrible war. Some modern practitioners of *seidr* suspect that the worship of Freyja, a name that simply means "Lady," has far more ancient roots among the reindeer-herding peoples of the Altai in Mongolia. In my efforts to research Her and come to know Her better, I learned that She was also considered a Goddess of magic, as fierce as She was passionate. Having struggled with low self-esteem all my life, I also noted that Freyja is known for teaching those who work with Her to cherish and value themselves. She is addressed by the honorific title, *Vanadis* (Lady of the Vanir), and is also known as the "Lady of the Bees."

A friend whose father had been a beekeeper needed a place for her hive while she and her husband moved from their rural home to one in town. I volunteered to host her bees and, through her, began to learn about these remarkable creatures. In time, we acquired hives of our own, and I often felt Freyja's presence when I worked with them.

On this mid-July morning at TwoTrees, the cicadas sing in sizzling seduction, a rhythmic counterpoint to the cuckoo calling from the creekside and the busy bickering of purple finches at the feeder. The cardinal family's latest chick, now well fledged, begs piteously from her father and older sister, although she is fully capable of cracking sunflower seeds for herself. I wonder how long they will indulge her. Through the open screen, I hear the low-pitched drone of one of our female hummingbirds, coming to drink from the well of nectar we provide, followed by sharp twittering as a male contests her right of place. On the nearby dining table, the cats chatter in excitement.

It will be hot again today — a temperature and humidity alien to my Norse and Germanic Ancestors — and I do not tolerate North Carolina summers well. I say a silent prayer to Surtr, primal God of fire, and ask that one of the Four Winds might come to balance His heat. For now, the boughs of beech and hemlock are utterly still.

Before the day grows unbearable, I slip into my sneakers and wander across the garden to the bee yard. The Monarda and lemon balm are rampant mounds, spilling over to block the paths, and it is clear that the Siberian iris will need to be thinned come fall. The sweet, even hum of the Little Sisters can be felt as well as heard. Even this early, they are about their tasks, coming and going from their lavender-painted hives with focus and a sense of purpose I admire.

Alpha hive has struggled for the past two years. Shaded longer in the morning, their hive warms later in the day, and they remain less robust. The Italian blonds who tend their Queen are larger, amber, and gold. Beta hive's Carniolans are fuzzy and more grayish, somewhat smaller but very diligent. Despite swarming in May, they draw out comb and make honey with remarkable efficiency, and we'll soon be able to harvest, thanks to their efforts.

Sunna crests the hill to the East and spills Her morning light all golden-green through the forest and then across the meadow. High against the pale aqua sky, a Red Tail Hawk soars, screaming its high shrill cry of joy.

"I see you, Brother," I say, and smile.

We placed a bench near the beeyard, watching them come and go, and made offerings of their wax and honey. In time, one hive swarmed and took up residence under my jewelry studio—a blessing from Freyja. While I was unable to hear their merry humming as I worked, I was aware of their industrious presence keeping me company. Conflicts with a belligerent neighbor led me to design a complex system of magical protective wards that used major trees around our land's perimeter as anchors and our bees as the wiring system.

During this time, nourished by nature, I created jewelry of great beauty and power, most of it now by commission, often incorporating strongly magical Celtic and Norse symbolism. From my bench, I gazed out through the blue-green boughs of the hemlocks northward toward the ancient Saura hills, listening to the wind and tides of birdsong. Just as nature had in my childhood, our land sheltered me, nurtured me, awakened me, accepted and healed me, teaching me to trust who I truly am.

Eleven
ACROSS THE WIDE WATER

On my mother's side, I am descended from the Scottish Reids, long associated with Clan Donnachaidh, a sept of Clan Robertson of Pitlochry, Perthshire. As a child, growing up in a family with a love for history and music, I heard many Scottish and Jacobite ballads and was often reminded that they represented a part of my family heritage. I learned them and sought out many more. The sound of bagpipes brought deep emotions and a lump in my throat. When I began to perform in Celtic bands, I gravitated to Scottish tunes and ballads, eventually learning to play the Scottish small harp.

As I sang the music of my forbearers, I often experienced a sense of inchoate longing, an inner ache the nature of which I could not articulate. Certain places called to me, especially dark Glencoe, Culloden's grim battlefield, and the ancient Standing Stones of Callanish on the Isle of Lewis, which I often dreamed of. I sought out books on Scotland and megaliths, and, when I thought of these places, I choked up, overcome with emotions I could not explain, flooded with what I can only describe as homesickness.

Although Eric and I had often talked about taking a trip to Scotland, I began to feel a sense of urgency about the plan. *Make this happen*, my inner Knowing advised.

Over the following year, I continued to research and plan, while feeling a growing sense that something important was to occur, although I had no clue what. Friends advised me to have faith and confidence that the Holy Powers would provide the knowledge of what I needed to accomplish in Scotland, along with the means to do so. In preparation, Eric and I decided to work a safe-travel spell, calling upon Freyr and

Freyja to lend Their protection.

In doing so, we had no idea what we were setting in motion.

As the time for travel drew closer, I prayed for the guidance and magical tools that would be needed, dreaming of a unique purple glass bowl with an interlaced design impressed into it. The following day, as we entered an antique show, I walked straight to a table where the bowl from my dream lay and made my purchase. I placed the bowl on the main house altar, nesting other items in it to build power. My pendulum and certain small stones and crystals that indicated they "wanted to go." I was reminded of the special clear quartz and amethyst crystals I'd been gifted long ago, carefully put aside for some then unforeseen purpose.

"These will be the keys," I was told, wondering what they would unlock.

The coincidences and synchronicities continued to flow, something I've always considered a sign that I am acting in alignment with the Holy Powers and in the Highest Good. Having been told that it often rains in Scotland, we put small umbrellas on the list of things to get, only to find folding umbrellas in the swag bags given to us at a friend's wedding. I worried about how to manage the care of our cats and a neighbor volunteered out of the blue to come over twice daily. Our B&B reservations fell into place, and the dream moved toward reality.

Divination indicated the possibility of blockages or obstacles, and I was encouraged to be adaptable. Shortly before the trip, I broke a toe. Meanwhile, a volcano in Iceland began to show signs of erupting, potentially interfering with air travel to or from Scotland. My heart-sister Kristy offered her magic to tame the fire mountain. We purchased travel insurance and could only pray while waiting to see what would happen.

Kristy's "dragon magic" worked—the volcano burped and then fell silent. We would indeed go to Scotland.

I experienced an overwhelming sense that there was some significant reason for this trip, something important I was being called to do, and, at the same time, I had no clear guidance on what that objective was.

On the Friday before we were to leave, I began to experience what I can best describe as a "download," receiving instructions from the Holy Powers on what I would need for the project I was being called to. I was instructed to create a pair of Portals: one in Scotland, the other at TwoTrees, the function of which was to create a magical bridge to allow the souls of homesick Scots who had died here in the New World to return to their beloved homeland. With that revelation came deep sobs and the relief of sure knowledge, quickly followed by a sense of wonder at being chosen to accomplish such a significant task—and the realization of how absurd the idea would sound to others.

I have lived a life filled with uncanny synchronicities and extraordinary experiences, but the trip to Scotland capped them all.

My Higher Guidance tells me this "bridge" will require a small amount of earth from both places and two very special crystals I've had for years. When I dowsed the small stones from my travel altar representing the Five Sacred Things (Earth, Air, Fire, Water, and Spirit), I was told to choose others instead. I also gathered tiny mirror-image quartz crystals, two small sastun (Mayan seeing stones), and a rare window crystal (one having seven terminal facets rather than the typical six thus associated with seeing into the past) which I intend to leave at Culloden. I am also directed to take a tuft

of Tristan's gray fur and a small Screech Owl feather, both being creatures of the "Between." Amber is sacred to Freyja; at noon, I was guided to take a pair of small amber pyramids, each about 10mm on the side and carved the rune Jera, *"Cycles," on their bottoms. Arranged point to point, the triangles form* Dagaz, *"Daybreak" or "Breakthrough." Side-by-side, they form* Berkana, *"New Beginning" or "Birth." Interestingly,* Dagaz *also represents stability between opposites, such as light and dark, stopping harmful energy but, at the same time, allowing good energy to slip through.*

At 7 a.m. on the third of September, after twenty hours of travel, we stumbled off the plane and into Scotland via the Glasgow airport, retrieved our luggage, and tried to figure out where to catch a bus into the city and our digs at the Kelvingrove Hotel on Sauchiehall Street. Although I've generally understood my Scottish friends with little problem, I'd always heard it said that Glaswegians have a particularly thick brogue. This proved true and made understanding the bus drivers quite challenging; and I'm sure they found our Southern drawls equally puzzling. We boarded and traveled through the suburbs and into the huge city, having no clue where we needed to go.

Glasgow is filled with amazingly beautiful old buildings, and we stared in wonder and delight. At some point, I realized we had overshot our stop and were headed back toward the way we'd come. After Eric managed to explain what we needed, our helpful driver actually stopped traffic in the midst of a busy thoroughfare to get us onto the correct bus for our hotel.

Although we arrived too early to check into our room, our host graciously allowed us to stash our luggage so that we could go out exploring unencumbered. We are just a few blocks from the Hunterian Art Gallery and several of the exhibits on Charles Rennie Macintosh that I wanted to see. So we crossed over the lovely Kelvin River and headed up a long hill through Kelvingrove Park. Upon arriving at the University of Glasgow, we discovered to our good fortune that it was Visitors Day, and, thus, many special activities were open at no charge. The University, founded in 1451, is one of Great Britain's four famed Ancient Universities, and we were awed by the gravitas and beauty of the old, ornate, red sandstone buildings.

Once recovered from the rigors of the long flight, we explored old Glasgow, shunning tourist spots to grab fish-and-chips with the locals and, later, to feast in a working-class pub surrounded by well-fueled noisy footballers.

I continued to wonder whether I would know what to do at Callanish. On the third morning, we picked up the rental we took to calling our "wee orange car" and headed northward over the huge Erskine Bridge spanning the Clyde. The smoky bulk of the Highlands rippled across the north, and we merged into the A82, which we later learned was considered one of the most dangerous roads in Britain—for good reason! Eric drove us north along the shore of Loch Lomond on a truly harrowing road—narrow, bumpy, winding, potholed, and with no shoulder whatsoever. We squeezed into oncoming traffic between the mountainside and the loch along with a bunch of mad Scotsmen driving lorries at 95 KPH.

The scenery was breathtaking, all dark water, lush forest, and cloud-checkered sky covering the countryside along the River Falloch, as we made our way toward the ancient seismic rift that cuts diagonally across Scotland from southwest to northeast. Eventually, the highway turned off and headed up into the high plateau of Rannoch Moor.

I immediately experienced a rush of strong emotion.

At first, the vales were broader and more open, sweeping upward through dark plantations of towering spruce, fir, and Scotch pines to the moor-covered hill-tops. With frequent pull-outs, we were able to stop often and take pictures of the unfolding land. All around us, craggy hills covered in bracken and heather stretched toward cloudy skies. The dark, bare mountains rose higher above the broad scree and heather-filled floodplains marked by thousands of meandering streams and small *lachan* (lakes), their slopes occasionally splattered with russet and gold as sunshine broke through the scudding clouds, revealing a deep blue sky above.

With every turn, the landscape seemed more familiar as we entered Glen Coe, whose name means "narrow valley." Here, the road swung northward. We crossed over the River Etive into a deep gorge formed by complex geological action and a long history of crustal uplift, volcanism, and glaciation. On our left rose dark Glencoe Mountain and the towering ramparts of Bidean nam Bian. To the right, across the River Coe, Anoach Eagach ridge.

We came to a turnout, and I asked to stop, awed by the stark beauty and filled with a strange mixture of sadness and homecoming. In my heart, I knew that Eric and I had lived in this valley in a prior lifetime before his death on Culloden's bloody moorland. One purpose of our trip had been to make peace with his untimely death, so long ago.

We followed a narrow trail over alluvial gravel and granite

boulders embedded in soggy peat, tussock grass, sedge, and heather to a small hill-top. The damp wind whistled around us, filled with whispering ghosts. Beneath our feet, the soil was scattered with bits of purplish rhyolite, red granite, and mica-flecked sandstone, so I asked for any stones that wished to come with me to call out. Beneath the unbelievably steep ramparts of some of Britain's highest mountains, sharp slopes of gold and russet and purple gorse, heather and bracken embraced sheltered vales of stunted hawthorn, wild roses, alders, and birches. The shifting clouds, occasionally dark with moisture, rode before the whipping wind, revealing an ever-changing vista filled with pooling water and a scrawl of tiny streams.

It came to me that rather than leaving the special "window" crystal on the battlefield of Culloden at the place of Eric's death, I wanted to place it in this beautiful place that had once been our home and a place of joy and life. I removed the water-clear stone from my pouch. Eric and I faced one another, hands clasped over the crystal as I said a few words of dedication. Then, I slipped it deep into the heart of a cairn of stones respectfully left by others through the years.

With charming accommodations in Ft. William as our base, we enjoyed a day trip on the "Hogwarts" steam train across the Highlands to the tiny coastal village of Maillaig, where we explored the harbor and enjoyed an encounter with a friendly harbor seal. On our way back to the train, we encountered a young woman tucked under a store-front awning playing beautiful traditional tunes on her small harp. I sat beside her, and we chatted during a break in the music. Remembering my own days as a hungry street musician, I left a generous tip in her bowl. That evening we feasted by the loch-side, dining sumptuously on freshly caught mussels and langoustines dripping in garlic butter, eating until we groaned.

The next morning, we drove north along Loch Lochy and Loch Oich and then for a long way, close beside the depths of Loch Ness, home of fabled Nessie. Eventually, we passed through Inverness, the city whose name means "Mouth of the River Ness," heading toward the battlefield of Culloden. Although there was no rain, the sky was dark and heavily overcast.

Knowing that friends had remarked on the intense emotional energies present at the Culloden battlefield, we had planned to shield ourselves ahead of time. This was overlooked until, approaching the site from the west, we were both struck with an overwhelming wave of loss and despair. We took a moment to prepare ourselves, then turned down the drive to the Visitor Center, where, to our delight and in another happy synchronicity, there was a Homecoming for the Clans celebration taking place, welcoming visitors to a variety of special activities. This was one of the many unexpected but happy coincidences which occurred during our trip.

Here, we encountered our first pipers, a pair of ramrod-straight men in full regimental kit who stood facing one another at the entry to the Center. We stood and listened for a while — tears blurred my eyes and a lump formed in my throat, as ever happens when I hear bagpipes. From there, we progressed out onto the battlefield: a broad, sloping moor crisscrossed with low fieldstone walls, hummocks of bracken and bogs, eerily silent but for the whistle of the wind. We walked hand-in-hand for a while along the pathway, stopping to read the various markers describing the locations of the Royalist and Jacobite troops. Here, on April 16, 1746, some 2000 exhausted and ill-commanded clansmen led by Bonnie Prince Charlie, Pretender to the throne of Scotland, were slaughtered by the forces supporting King Charles II, commanded by William Augustus, Duke of Cumberland.

Prior to the trip, I had wondered whether, as intuitive as I am, I would sense where Eric had fallen in that lifetime. At some point, my attention continued to be drawn to an overgrown stone wall that ran northeastward along the Jacobite forces' placement. After trying to ignore the tug I felt, I left the path and set off through the boggy field toward the wall with Eric in tow. As I drew closer, I did indeed have clear knowledge of the place of his death, seeing the event clearly as if viewing a film loop; however, I wanted Eric to identify this himself, and I even went so far as to walk up a little ways, aiming to throw him off.

Instead, he stopped abruptly at that point and muttered, "Whoa! That's it."

I went to him, and we embraced tearfully. Together, we placed a beautiful piece of amethyst, a stone that strengthens spiritual connections, in the turf next to the wall to honor that life. Proceeding around the battlefield, we eventually came to the mass graves for the various major clan groups and the cairn-like monument to the fallen Jacobites. I left a small bouquet of yellow and purple wildflowers on the stone honoring the Atholl Highlanders with whom my Reid ancestors had fought.

After a long drive northeast across the dark, rolling Highlands to the ferry port of Ullapool, we found our B&B. Here, we were to face one more obstacle. We had somehow failed to reserve our space on the huge ferry that would transport us from the Scottish mainland to the Isle of Lewis, and we arrived in Ullapool only to learn we would be on standby, with no assurance we could cross.

Once again I frantically texted Kristy, and she set about her spellwork to open the way. We were to be the final vehicle allowed on the boat the following morning!

Twelve
THE BRIDGE OF SOULS

The morning was brisk and bright, our long ferry ride to the Outer Hebrides accompanied by a phalanx of dusky dolphins — surely a good sign. As the dark waters rolled beneath us, I thought back to my Viking ancestors who raided and then settled these islands, contributing to the braided heritage I carry.

Once on the island, we grabbed lunch and found a laundromat. Later, as we drove south on the Isle of Lewis, the trees and gardens of Stornoway gave way to moorland, rough pasture, bare stone, and water everywhere, in thousands of streams, pools, and *lachan*. The narrow two-lane road became one lane and then a gravel track across the rolling wilderness of peat bogs and harvestings. The closer we drew to Callanish, the more my excitement grew. Before I could ever see the Stones, I felt them like a beacon. Then we crested a rise and crossed a wide swale: I spotted them, silhouetted against the sky, their jagged forms as familiar to me as my own face.

Within a mile, we saw the sign for the croft where we would be staying and turned down the willow-hedged drive, pulling up behind the simple modern house that would be our home base for the next two nights. Our host, a native of the island, was a tall, plain-spoken, gregarious man in his mid-sixties. After giving us a brief tour of the place and sharing a bit about his sustainable approach to farming, he asked directly what was of primary interest to us so that he could best help and benefit us during our stay.

"The Stones!" we replied.

He smiled and gestured to an elderly woman working intently at the dining room table. "Well, you've timed it perfectly. That woman is Margaret Curtis, and she is probably THE world's greatest authority on the stones and their historical and astronomical context. She's compiling all of her earlier work into a major volume. We have her staying here with us instead of at her place, because, otherwise, she'd forget to eat or rest!"

It turned out that he had been the maintenance superintendent for the site for thirty years and had assisted Ms. Curtis in the excavations. The universe could not have guided us to a more perfect base, and, as a geomancer, I could hardly wait to experience what the Ancients had accomplished.

Our host unrolled a map and pointed out numerous megalithic and bronze age sites on the island, including two other groups of standing stones nearby. The giant stones of Callanish One are arranged roughly like a Celtic cross, with paired avenues of smaller stones running north and south, single rows of stones extending east and west, a central circle of larger slabs surrounding the foundation of a burial cairn, and an enormous center stone. The subtle energies and magic of so many ancient sites have been disrupted, whether by archaeologists, religious fanatics, or locals salvaging stone for construction projects. Although Callanish One has seen multiple excavations, they had clearly been done carefully, and I was amazed by the power and music present in this grouping.

Over 5,000 years ago, each stone had been quarried from a plateau eleven miles to the north and shaped with intention, then dragged on log rollers across rough and boggy ground. Many were chosen for their graphic components and danced with inclusions of hornblende and quartz. Wide bands of pink feldspar suggested images on the huge gneiss slabs, the largest of which is almost thirty feet long and four feet wide.

After settling into our pleasant room overlooking the standing stones, Eric and I crossed the short span of moorland to explore this place I'd been called to. Dropping into a light trance, I became aware of streams of blue and gold light arching intermittently from the tip of one stone to another. The energy of the western arm of the stones was especially strong; when I stood at the end, I felt almost pushed westward, toward the Atlantic.

It was there my Knowing told me I was to open the first Portal, a magical gateway between Scotland and America. Dowsing with my pendulum indicated the stones were alternately positive and negative in their polarity, and I found that I wanted to walk back and forth through that western arm, weaving in and out between them.

I still wondered how I was supposed to accomplish my sacred task. The download was clear, but not very specific. As I shared my uncertainty with my husband, he calmly assured me that I would know. "You've done what you were told to do, made the trip, brought the stuff. Honey, you've got this!"

Tonight, the most remarkable thing happened! As the long twilight drew on, most of the visitors left, apart from one other couple. The woman brought a green stone to the center of the circle and touched it reverently to the central monolith. Then, with the stone in her left hand, she took a rattle from her bag and began to walk to each stone in turn, speaking softly to them and kissing them.

I realized that she was a fellow spirit worker, and so I stepped back out of the circle's energy pattern to give her space. I'd been standing out to the northwest for about five minutes, just watching, when she beckoned me to come closer.

I replied that I was just giving her room to work.

"You need to come into the Circle," she insisted. "The stones want you here, and you can handle the energy."

Knowing that the Holy Powers had provided all sorts of resources for this trip and the Portal work, I smiled and went toward her. She took me by the arm and led me over to the entrance to the central roofless burial chamber, which I had previously avoided entering.

"Just get comfortable," she said. "The stones will do their work."

So, I knelt in the chamber with my forehead resting on the pouch containing my crystals and tools which I cradled in my hands on the circle's true center stone. I prayed that the working would be accomplished in the highest good of all and felt a deep healing peace.

After asking Eric to step back out of the circle, which he did, the woman began to chant softly, using her rattle and weaving the energies of the stones around me. I sang with her in wordless harmony.

After some time, she touched the crown of my head to let me know that she had finished, and I thanked the Gods for her gift. She had attuned my subtle energies to those of the stones in preparations for the Portal work during the following night's full Moon.

I rose and embraced her, expressing my gratitude, noting that the arcs of energy spanning between the great stones were now a uniform violet.

The following morning, stuffed with a grand breakfast of free-range eggs, Stornoway black pudding, home-cured bacon and sausage, buttery scones, and home-made jam, we made a brief stop at the Visitor Center and then explored other sites nearby. The first, Callanish Two, comprised of five or so broad, shorter stones, proved energetically inert, and I had the sense that someone had intentionally disabled it. I felt sufficiently uncomfortable there that I chose not to enter.

Callanish Three, located on a nearby rise facing Callanish One, remains energetically intact, despite several missing stones. To the south rose a low mound, much like the one at Callanish One. This time I felt called to touch and caress the stones and, without realizing it, began to sing softly and intuitively to myself. This carried me into a deep place, and I just went with it, focusing on how I felt rather than what I was doing.

Of particular note was the tall western stone, blatantly phallic in shape. I stood for some time near it, understanding that it was an honoring of the potency of the God of the Wild Things and the fertility of the Great Mother. I laid my palm upon its softly striated face and knew without question that it had previously been offered blood and was hungry.

I shared this awareness with Eric, and we agreed to use a diabetic lancet to offer it a gift of ours. I have learned to honor such promptings.

That evening, the sky was heavily overcast and the wind sharp, so we both dressed warmly and returned to the Stones around seven. While the cloud cover did not interfere with the energy we required, it was disappointing not to be able to see the moon rise through the monoliths. I walked among the stones for some time, continuing to sing softly as I had earlier in the day. This singing helped me shift into the altered state I required for our working. Even then, there were many people coming and going, including a number of photographers jockeying for shots.

I eventually made the decision to move to the south of the circle and sat down on a stone outside of the alignment to await a prompting from Higher Guidance that it was time for me to work. At that point, I still had only the most general idea of what might be involved in opening the portal and continued to pray for guidance. "I don't know how to do this!" I said. "I'm here. I'm willing. I brought the stuff You told me to. But, I have no clue how I'm actually supposed to make a Portal for a spirit bridge!"

Eric walked around a bit and eventually came to sit beside me. Our hope was that as it grew later and colder, perhaps the others present would leave. Gradually, they all did—with the exception of a pair of lovers who sat down together with their backs against the outermost stone of the circle's western arm, exactly where I needed to work.

It became evident that they had no intention of leaving, and I expressed concern about what to do. It was then that Eric suggested that we check out an area just beyond the westernmost stone where the hill dropped off rather abruptly into a rocky face with a narrow path below. The energy was good there, still strongly westward in its flow, and, while we were aligned directly with the western arm of the circle, we were down below where the other visitors could see us. Nothing for it but to just go for it and trust that what my gut told me to do would be appropriate.

The dusk deepened as I laid out my altar on a small flat area embraced by the exposed rock face. I gathered a few pinches of the dark, peaty earth and placed them in a pouch. Then, I took out the first mirror crystal and the luminous sastun. Strangely, although I knew I'd packed both amber pyramids, only one was now present. I assumed that the Holy Powers had already selected one to remain in Scotland and so kept the remaining one for the second Portal. I tucked the little mirror crystal and sastun into a cleft in the rocks as an offering and link.

Eric, who had agreed to act as my energetic anchor, stood in the north, place of Elemental Earth and stability. I stood in the south, place of Elemental Fire and creative force. We clasped hands and took several cleansing breaths then centered ourselves. Then, I made a statement of intent, setting forth what we hoped to accomplish. Speaking softly, I hallowed the space and called upon Freyja and Freyr to aid the working. As I turned my back to the Stones and faced westward toward America, a sharp wind blew from the north.

At that high latitude, days are long, even into September, but, by 10 p.m., the overcast sky loomed a deep purple-gray. Out on the bay, fishing boats plied the dark waters, their lamps twinkling. Across the water, the mountains formed the dark silhouette of a sleeping woman, another element in the landscape revered by local ancient people.

I felt so blessed to be present in a landscape so long held sacred. "Holy Ones," I prayed, "guide my heart and hand to do Your work."

It came to me to sing a particular haunting air I've always loved. I opened my heart, and the music came forth, carrying me into deep trance. I moved into the archaic melody I'd been channeling earlier in the day, using the chant to gather energy and to focus my consciousness on accomplishing the first part of this great working. I grounded deeply and gathered energy.

Using the long clear quartz crystal in my right hand, I drew the first Portal, marking an arched doorway in space before me. While the dark landscape was visible through that doorway once I completed it, all around it were thousands of tiny soft lights, like fuzzy white stars or fireflies.

I transferred that crystal to my left hand, and still singing, used the large amethyst to draw an invoking sigil. It felt to me that my heart burst open and a huge arc of light exploded from my chest and on through the Portal to cross the Atlantic.

For some moments, I stood, suspended and swaying in the energy flow, my voice soaring higher and higher to end on one pure *tone that hung in the gloaming. I have no idea how long I remained frozen in place, but, eventually, I turned to Eric, and he helped me shuffle to the altar to close the ritual and gather our things.*

I had established the first Portal.

Thirteen
HOMEWARD

Upon our return to TwoTrees, the gathering spirits of the Dead filled the land, eager to make use of the Bridge of Souls once it was complete. It had originally been my plan to open the second Portal in the upper *Ve* here at TwoTrees in conjunction with the full Moon of October 8. As the date approached, Higher Guidance made clear that the timing and location were both wrong. After consultation with wise friends and intensive divination, I decided the second working should wait until the naturally occurring thinning of the veil at Samhain, which some call Halloween, a time long dedicated to the honoring of the Dead.

Dividing my focus and energy between the time-stream where I held my link with the open Portal in Scotland and, simultaneously, my need to function in currently elapsing time, I grew increasingly fatigued, agitated, and scattered. The sensation of holding the connection that would be used to open the second Portal and anchor the bridge reminded me of singing a sustained high note without the opportunity to breathe. It required more and more energy to hang on to that connection as time passed.

As with the details of the first Portal working, I had much uncertainty and confusion over what to do and when to do it. Eric and I discussed moving the timing up to the new Moon on October 23, occurring in conjunction with a partial solar eclipse. Divination remained unclear. However, we were in agreement that the site for the second Portal should be shifted to the area of the lower *Ve*, located between moving water and the exposed rocky cliff face of our bluff—a space we had dedicated as sacred to Lady Hel, the Norse Goddess of the Dead.

On the afternoon of Wednesday, October 22, intuiting that I would receive further guidance, I felt prompted to go down to the lower *Ve*. Along with a folding chair and my iPhone for music, I carried a small bag containing a pen, notebook, and my runes.

My Higher Guidance tells me that I should bury the small crystals along with the combined earths from our land and from Callanish in the natural cave formed by the roots of the big linden tree at the point of the land facing east and up-stream.

As soon as I entered the woods, I found my consciousness began to shift, and I could feel the inclination of the energy pushing to make connection. I sat down with my back to the huge tree which symbolizes our World Tree — the axis of earth and heaven — and internally centered myself to create Sacred Space. I called upon Freyr and Freyja and the spirits of the Ancestors to attend me, and I sank deep, feeling and seeing the Dead gathered behind me, awaiting permission to cross. I could also feel the presence of both of my parents: my father standing to my left with his hand resting lightly across my shoulders and my mother to my right, gently stroking my hair. This was the first time since their deaths that I had felt them both present with me at the same time, and I wept — carried along in the deeply moving energy of the music of which I was a part. In an arc before me sat the beloved cats who are buried at TwoTrees. Knowing that cats are sacred to Freyja, I smiled.

With my inner sight, I could see the dark disc of the Moon sliding toward the Sun, which I visualized as being directly overhead, until it centered itself against that light. At that moment of the vision, the annular ring of Sunna's light streamed down all around me, surrounding me in an inverted bowl of opalescent, luminous energy.

Next, I cast my thoughts to Scotland. As it had the night of the first Portal opening at Callanish, a strong, cold north wind blew toward me, offering a kinesthetic memory to help carry me into that other reality. There, I once again stood at twilight, clearly visualizing the tall stones in their ancient alignment. I turned slowly, recalling the panoramic image of their dark shapes silhouetted against the shadowed countryside. I stepped into the small tomb and knelt. Then, rose to lay my face against the cold surface of the heart stone.

I felt that the energies were such that the second Portal was ready to open and bridge right then. Yet, I had none of the tools required with me.

With mixed feelings, I began to withdraw myself somewhat from the building tide of energy. I asked to be shown the specifics for the working and drew the rune Laguz as a guide rune, representing water and flow. Then, with some significant effort, I gave thanks and brought my consciousness back to the present, noting that the wind paused with me and then reversed directions.

In keeping with the instructions I had been given and trusting to my inner Knowing, I gathered the tools required in addition to those items brought back from the first Portal opening in Scotland. I polished a large copper bowl given to me long ago, filled a small bottle with a dram of good Scotch and washed a pottery bowl that had been one of Eric's first gifts to me. In addition, I took a small skein of rainbow-painted yarn given to me by my heart-sister, Kristy. All of these items went into an old Cherokee basket handed down from my mother's mother. I also picked the season's last yellow marigolds from the garden, knowing that many cultures use them to honor the Dead.

At about 4:00 p.m., I took my chair and the basket and walked along the path to the large raised sandstone slab that serves as Hel's hörgr (or altar), where I sat for some time reconnecting to the energies still present from the day before, while also recalling the panoramic image of Callanish and the night of the first Portal opening. Eric walked down from the upper Circle at 5:45 p.m.. We embraced silently, then joined hands to ground and center before I made the statement of intent.

Eric clambered over the rocks to dip water from the stream with the copper bowl. Facing each direction, we hallowed the space, and then I consecrated salt and water in the copper bowl, adding whisky. We invoked the presences of Freyr and Freyja and offered libations to the Ancestors. Turning to face the *hörgr*, I emptied the bags of mica-flecked red clay from TwoTrees and fibrous black peat from Callanish into the pottery bowl, stirring to combine them before moistening the mixture with more whisky. I scooped part of the mud into a palm-sized abalone shell and added the *sastun*, crystals, and a small yellow leaf that spiraled down to settle on top.

Raising my hands in blessing as I had at Callanish, once again I sang. When the song was done, I took up the skein of yarn, my crystals, and the abalone shell. Eric carried the bowl of enchanted water and followed me out to the Portal point.

I temporarily rested the yarn and key crystals beside me while I buried the shell filled with the mixed earths, small crystal, and engraved amber deep in the sprawling roots of the Freya's linden tree. I stood, facing east toward Scotland, and spoke over the water, at the same time visualizing myself standing on the twilit hilltop at Callanish six weeks previously. With a swooping motion, I slung the water out of the bowl and upward in a great arc — where it seemed to hang for a timeless moment before splashing back into the stream. I looped one end of the yarn around my wrist and handed the rest of the skein to Eric along with the then-empty bowl. He moved back to his seat at our World Tree, played out the multicolored yarn, a reminder of Bifröst, the rainbow bridge of Norse mythology, and of the support of my magical sisters, all fiber workers.

As I had at Callanish, I sang intuitively until the energy felt right, then delineated the Portal using the long, clear crystal. With the phantom amethyst, I drew the invoking sigil. The pressure of the many Dead behind me, striving to close the gap between the active Portals, quickly became overwhelming. I raised my arms to open my heart center and the energy burst through me in a rainbow arc of light soaring eastward to Scotland, completing the bridge.

My part done, I lowered my arms and stood softly weeping, swaying in the flood of grateful, home-bound souls. The completion of this sacred task opened something within me, deepening the connection I felt with our land and the many Beings who share it with us. I came to understand that spirits exist in a logical hierarchy. Seed, leaf, twig, branch, and tree have spirits, although that of the tree is far more aware than that of the smaller components. Then, there is the spirit that governs each individual species (holly, red oak, shagbark hickory, tulip poplar) and that which governs each family (the Oaks, the Pines, the Beeches). Greater still, the Grandfather or governing spirit of all deciduous trees, so very different in their natures than the more ancient evergreens.

In the same way, I learned to recognize the tiny sleeping spirits of pebbles and stones, larger spirits of boulders and outcrops, the great spirits of mountains, and, larger yet, those of whole mountain ranges and other grand features of the living earth—valleys, arroyos, canyons, gorges. Water spirits also range from the tiniest droplet sparkling in mist or dew to puddles, trickles, rivulets, streams, ponds, lakes, and seas, each with a unique consciousness and character—and some more conscious than others.

This understanding put me in a humble place and reinforced the necessity of relationship in all shamanic working. I was not working alone. I was only able to achieve this extraordinary accomplishment with the assistance of and in relationship with other Beings, both Human and Non-Human. The Holy Powers that directed me to undertake such an implausible task made sure that the necessary tools found their way to me. Through their action, my path intersected with the paths of others who played significant roles in this undertaking. They removed blockages and shifted circumstances to reinforce my confidence and to facilitate our travel and accommodations.

As I reflected, I realized that significant to this experience – and to my personal journey – was the development of faith, of trust. My lived experience had taught me to trust the spiritual messages that came through prayer, through divination, through personal revelation, even when such messages instructed me to do things that seemed puzzling or absurd. At the same time, I was learning the discernment to tease apart those messages from random impulses or fantasies. I had developed faith that the things I was being guided to do were meaningful and helped to bring the world around me into greater balance.

The numerous synchronicities that graced the whole process of creating the Bridge of Souls affirmed for me not only the rightness of my own skills and instincts. Participating in this extraordinary event also affirmed my sacred connection within the larger web of creation. This accomplishment was a central aspect of my *Wyrd* in this lifetime—the meaning of my life work in relationship with the Holy Powers. I was—and am—deeply grateful and filled with wonder. This is who I am.

Whatever we do affects the Whole, whether or not we, ourselves, can perceive the impact of our actions. We are always collaborating with others, and through such collaboration, all are enriched. Hail the Holy Powers!

I am restless today, feeling agitated and unfocused. My heart tells me I need water, earth, sunlight — things that so often call me home to my Self. The morning is still reasonably cool, especially in the deep shade of the hemlocks and beeches that cloak the bluff here at TwoTrees. I take my shaman's staff, knowing three legs are always steadier than two, and my tobacco pouch, in case I want to make a small offering to some forest spirit.

Even from the front steps, I hear the merry hum of our bees, the Little Sisters coming and going in their endless search for nectar and pollen. Near them, rosy Monarda, bee balm, sways in the breeze, and I can see the buds on the catnip that will soon offer a treat to our bees and cats alike. I head down the trail winding past the weeping cherry tree where we leave offerings to golden Freyr, the Norse God of fertility and good will.

In the upper Ve, I stop to gaze up at the sky, pale turquoise with scattered clouds. This worship space is marked out by fat sections of pine logs and lush ferns that frame standing stones marking the four *directions. A dragonfly comes to investigate me, hovering at eye level before zipping away, and I hear the calls of finches and warblers. The laughing cry of the juvenile woodpecker who frequents our feeder echoes through the high woods. Before I continue, I remove a pinch of sweetly fragrant tobacco and place it on the altar, offering thanks to my Gods and the spirits of the land.*

The trail down to Town Fork Creek is narrow and steep, established by deer many years ago. I place my feet carefully, as much to avoid stepping on the plants as to keep from tripping. In a few minutes, I find myself on the gravel bed left by many years of erosion and high water, the multicolor pebbles beneath my feet once part of the quartzite bluff our home rests on. The stream is fat and muddy, thanks to recent rains. The water swirls and sparkles in the dappled sunlight breaking through the tree canopy, and the susurration of wind and splashing water draws a peace into my heart, as I stand in a dreamlike state.

Sweep me clean, Holy Powers, I pray.

Fourteen
TO DIE AND RISE AGAIN

Not long after we'd returned from Scotland, I heard that Northern Tradition shaman Raven Kaldera was looking for sacred smiths to make components for a magical shamanic breastplate. I immediately contacted him and was engaged to create the segment dedicated to Freyr as Lord of Ljóssálfheim, realm of the Light Elves. The chevron of bright silver would be pierced with dozens of leaf silhouettes and set with an oval of moss agate. Raven would pay for the necessary silver and agreed to spend several intensive days with us during his next teaching tour, fielding my questions in recompense for my labor.

At the same time, uncertainty loomed. I had noticed a lump in my neck. Recalling how my mother's cancer had first shown itself, I asked my doctor to have me checked. In May of 2015, I underwent a needle biopsy that revealed I had papillary cancer of the thyroid. My age and the fact that the cancer had metastasized to nearby lymph nodes made me a Stage IV high-risk patient. In July, I underwent a seven-hour surgery to remove my entire thyroid, two of my four parathyroids, and eleven adjacent lymph nodes. At first I recovered well, but I was soon readmitted to the hospital with life-threateningly low calcium levels.

There, nine days after surgery, the doctors struggled to stabilize me as I slipped toward death. I was aware of their urgent whispered conversation as my consciousness filled with bright light and white noise. I realized that I was dying. While I felt sad for Eric and my boys, I also felt quite calm in this Knowing.

In the midst of this experience, I was visited by the Goddess Freyja. She tenderly assured me that all was well, as She began the work of disassembling me, making numerous adjustments, and then rewiring me with shining golden threads. Above the crown of my head, She placed what looked to me like a big satellite dish, preparing me for deeper shamanic work. Feeling safe in Her hands and totally at peace in Her care, I drifted into sleep. This dismemberment and remaking is a classic feature of what defines a traditional shaman in many cultures.

The following morning, my calcium levels were stable again.

Eric brought me home to TwoTrees to heal and nursed me tenderly. I camped on the couch or our bed, constantly attended by my Tristan who positioned his soft, silvery body on my chest, heart to heart, streaming unconditional love and gazing at me through his beautiful half-closed, gold-green eyes. I had been advised that I would feel fatigue as my body adjusted to supplemental medication.

Still, nothing prepared me for the hypersensitivity resulting from my near death ordeal—and that certainly wasn't something I could discuss with my doctors. Freyja appeared in dreams to teach me how to adjust the level of sensory input by closing my new "receiver" like a camera aperture.

"I've been with you all along," She assured me one afternoon when I was struggling—and I recalled the shining lady who used to perch on the foot of my bed when I was a frightened child. As I grew up, I concluded that I had imagined Her. But now, Freyja was assuring me that assumption was wrong.

In late August, Raven came to TwoTrees for several days. A transgender activist, author, and controversial force in the Norse Pagan community, he is owned by the Norse Death Goddess, Hel. Much of what I knew at that time about the Northern Traditions, I had learned from Raven's many books — texts that combined his own unique experiences with accounts from other practitioners in this tradition.

The Norse Sagas and Eddas, our primary source of information about this culture, were once part of a rich oral tradition. These stories and tales were not written down until several hundred years after the Viking Era when they were recorded by Christianized Norse monks who were primarily interested in them as examples of beautiful, poetic language rather than as historical accounts. Coupled with old-school archaeology done by scholars with cultural biases, these tales became the foundation of a skewed, romanticized vision used by some to reinforce an agenda of racial purity and superiority. Subsequent scholarship has revealed a culture that was, in reality, both diverse and surprisingly inclusive.

As the first person I was to meet with the same rare endocrine condition I have, Raven was to help me better understand the gender dysphoria I have struggled with throughout my life. I was also to learn that many of those called into service by the Norse Gods as spirit workers in present times are LGBTQI, and that many suffer from chronic illnesses, are neurodivergent, have compromised immune systems, migraines, and strange food sensitivities. We also share a history of trauma, as if the Gods use it to break us open to Their will. Or, perhaps, it is the empathy and sensitivity that can flow from trauma that make us especially useful to the Gods.

As we talked, Raven assured me that many of the very things I found so bewildering and curious about my life and work seemed to be common among traditional shamans and spirit workers. He also shared his vision of a Northern Shamanism Guild offering rigorous training in an effort to establish a body of competent service professionals. The training system he described consisted of a novice pre-level and, then, three subsequent levels for training individuals called as shamanic practitioners. After the third level, those, like myself who had undergone the classic shamanic death and dismemberment and were God-Owned would undergo the challenge of an initiation ordeal to become shamans, and, if successful, additional levels of training by the spirits. While I knew of no historical evidence for such a system, Raven's Guild would definitely address a need.

Raven indicated that training might take many years and could even be the work of a lifetime. He also spoke candidly of the life-or-sanity-threatening illnesses that can plague individuals who resist the calling of the Gods. We scheduled semi-annual visits. In between, I would complete challenging exercises and document my work, with the occasional phone call thrown in. Between Raven's books and our conversations, I had the impression that the Northern Tradition community was broad and thriving and that the Guild was already a well-established organization.

We spoke of the differences between the personal empowerment focus of Michael Harner's Core Shamanism and the classical shamanism Raven practiced, which focuses on a life of service to a community within a specific cultural context. In the case of the Northern Traditions, which derive from cultures lacking written history, there is little intact lineage. As in many traditional cultures, a shaman may be trained independently by the spirits who have called them and without any other human mentor's involvement. We borrow a term from the Buryat Mongols who refer to those who are spirit taught as *bagshagui*. More is discerned by the study of archaeological evidence and more through personal revelation, often referred to as Unverified Personal Gnosis or UPG. When multiple individuals independently intuit the same information, it becomes Shared Personal Gnosis or Verified Personal Gnosis; in effect, peer-corroborated knowledge.

On our second day together, Raven guided me through a meditation in which, after entering a trance, we shapeshifted into our flying forms. I followed him on a tour of the inner energetic landscape. He also scanned me in preparation for the healing I'd requested, so that he had a better sense of what he needed to do. I could tell he was drained from the prior day and offered to take him down to our lower *Ve,* a space dedicated to Lady Hel, where he could ask our *landvaettir* — land spirits — for some energy. Since we have our own World Tree and do our work with the Dead and the Underworld there, it seemed perfect for him.

Raven sang to the land. Then, I sang to him. As we followed the path back along the stream and then up the hill, he seemed more present. A gifted herbalist, he was quick to point out medicinal plants as we passed them and to ask about those unfamiliar to him which caught his eye.

After lunch and a rest, he walked me through the use of the "Soul Map," a tool given to him by revelation representing the aspects of the human soul as understood in this tradition. He had me close my eyes and draw tumbled stones from a gourd bowl as he called out the name of each aspect of the soul. Depending on what I had drawn, he could discern whether I had low, average, or ample resources for that aspect, was blocked somehow or aided by the Gods. That reading was followed up by having me draw runes from his pouch for each point. Their nature and position gave him additional insight and detail. He also drew extra runes for clarification. He was able to counsel me on some things I needed to work on and, also, seemed pleasantly surprised by some of what was revealed.

It was increasingly clear that I was being called into service to the community.

On my way out to my studio to get something Raven had

asked for, I noticed a cluster of red and white fly agaric mushrooms, also known as *Amanita muscaria*, around our backyard fire pit. These iconic fungi were one of the first entheogenic plants to be used by ancient shamans and are a treat much loved by reindeer. On my way back to the house, the *vaet* or spirit of the fungi, sometimes referred to as Little Red Man, spoke to me and told me to pick him. I selected the cap he indicated and brought it into the house, placing it on our main house altar to honor the Northern spirits. I had read that this *vaet* was garrulous and difficult, often sharp and demanding, but that was not how I experienced him. There was a curious sense of familiarity about this fungi, and I recalled my childhood spirit encounter with "Mr. Mushroom."

That afternoon, at my request, Raven agreed to do a healing on the area of my now-missing thyroid. I was especially concerned with how the surgery and upcoming radiation treatment might impact my singing voice.

With the air electric from an impending thunderstorm, I got "whammied" — Raven's favorite word for the use of magical power toward some goal. We set up my massage table in the center of the greatroom, and I lay on it with my bundle of sacred tools on the floor beneath me, my horse bone wand between my shins and my forging hammer between my breasts. Raven sang over me and cleansed me with mugwort smoke (the Northern equivalent of sage). He marked runes over my scar in red ocher, then galdred or entoned the runes Cweorth (which cauterizes) and Os, sacred to Bragi, the God of bards and skalds.

The experience was electric and remarkable.

Curiously, when the healing was done, the spirit of Little Red Man came and stood at my feet, telling me, "You've passed the test and will walk the roads with me."

When I told Raven about this, he raised an eyebrow and looked at me intently.

I wondered, What test?

We took another break so Raven could eat and rest. When he got up, he surprised me by offering me an apprenticeship. "When you have apprentices or students of your own, will you promise you'll pass on the knowledge so that it won't be lost?" he solemnly asked.

The importance of recovering and preserving ancient wisdom resonated deeply with me, and I impulsively said yes. Cancer and my brush with death made me feel isolated and vulnerable. I hungered for something meaningful to focus on. That Raven felt I had the strength to walk this unquestionably difficult road was gratifying. Moreover, I felt Seen and Understood — and that is seductive.

In retrospect, I should have taken time to consider the invitation further.

Having worked with excellent teachers and mentors and having undergone several life-transforming initiations, I welcomed the potential for such an experience in the context of the Northern Traditions. At that point, my knowledge of Norse culture and lore was relatively limited. Wanting to "do it right," I put aside my prior alliances, skills, and way of working to start over from scratch.

To be clear, this was not something Raven asked of me — and, in many ways, it was a decision that would complicate my apprenticeship and my relationship with him. In retrospect, I realize that I did both of us a disservice by discounting my many years of lived experience, knowledge, and skill. The

apprenticeship I committed to turned out to be deeply challenging, as I balanced learning new skills with the gradual
realization that I was called to a different understanding of the
Northern Traditions than Raven. I would ultimately have to
find my own way.

In September, I underwent the second stage of my cancer
treatment, swallowing radioactive iodine intended to kill any
stray cancerous thyroid cells left after my thyroidectomy. That
procedure was followed up by five days of isolation in our
guest room so I did not inadvertently irradiate my husband
and our cats. This "death" in my old life rippled outward.

While my immediate family stayed connected, no one else
called to check on me, brought casseroles, or volunteered to
drive me to checkups. It was as if, to the outer world and most
of those I had considered "friends," I simply ceased to exist.
Terrible fatigue and brain fog made it difficult for me to do
anything productive. My limited resources were focused on
healing and the shamanic training I'd finally begun.

I rested and my vivid dreams were filled with images of
longships reflected in the still waters of a fjord, of a tall woman with wheaten hair and cool grey eyes who called me to
walk with her through the long grass of her brother's orchard.
I wondered, *Were they dreams of remembering or foreshadowing?*

In the months afterwards, the spirit of Little Red Man became a significant presence and ally. Curiously, he appeared
much like a garden gnome, with a pointed red hat and full
white beard. At his direction, I sewed a bag of red and tan
suede painted with the primitive image of a reindeer. I placed
the now-dried *Amanita* cap within it. One evening, feeling
blocked, I decided to take the pouch to bed with me and to
ask Red Man for guidance. I held the bag against my heart for
a while and spoke silently to him, then placed the bag on the

headboard of the bed above me. Almost immediately, I began to have a vision.

Initially, we were seated on the ground, knee to knee, in a small clearing in an old-growth conifer forest. Little Red Man was somewhat smaller than me, but had a strong presence. He gazed at me with his sharp, black eyes. There was a soft glow around us but no obvious light source.

He spoke, "The Roads are there. They are always there if you know how to look."

Suddenly, we were both very small, and I found myself thinking of Alice in Wonderland *when Alice takes the pill and shrinks. I looked around us and realized that what had seemed like trackless forest was, in fact, threaded by thousands of little trails and paths made by mice and shrews and other wee creatures.*

"Look up!" he urged, and I saw the full Moon shining down through the trees. I glanced back at him and saw that he was mounted on a mouse. As he turned and galloped away into the forest, he called out, "Just look up... then look down."

I felt an upward surge and shifted into Screech Owl form, rising through the fragrant pine boughs, flying northward. In my head I heard, "No, no! That won't be nearly enough! Try again..."

With another surge, I shifted into the form of a Great Gray Northern Owl (a creature I'd never become before) and felt the lengthening of my wings and the greater power of their beats. In the far distance, beyond the taiga, I could see the wide expanse of snowy tundra, and, above all, the shimmering curtains of the aurora. Eventually, I came to where I looked down upon a herding camp with the tents glowing merrily from the fires within. Nearby, reindeer were bedded down, and, around them, the snow sparkled under the bright face of the Moon. I settled "into" a big cow, warm in my thick winter coat, happily chewing my cud, aware of the low humming grunts of the other members of the herd around me. Contentment.

As I slipped away into sleep, Little Red Man spoke again. "Your batteries are depleted. You need to take time to walk the woods, re-connect with the land, recharge yourself. Go and walk. You'll see."

I made time the following afternoon to wander down by the creek, and I was fortunate enough to see our resident heron, like a living dinosaur, busily searching the shallows for min-nows. Seated with my back against the rock face of the cliffs, I studied the rich environment around me filled with my fellow residents at TwoTrees: lichens and mosses and ferns, wild ginger and hepatica, mountain laurel bushes and mixed hard-woods. Butterflies sipped mineral-rich water from the damp sands, and I laughed in delight as an electric green kingfisher shot from a branch to spear a frog, startling the much larger heron. Little Red Man was right: the land and its many Beings always recharged me. I gratefully resolved to do all I could to strengthen my relationship with this ancient, magical spirit.

Often, just as I hover between waking and sleeping, I am visited by Little Red Man, mounted on his reindeer. He has taught me a song to call him and is pleased when I sing it.

Grandfather Redcap, for so shall I hail Thee!
Friend of my fathers, my teacher and guide—
Take not my life as the price for your wisdom.

Carry me safely as I seeking go.
Far-Seer, Fair-Flyer, come with me, cleanse my eyes.
Lift me up, let me see
Let me know now.

Last night, I saw Reindeer standing in crisp snow in front of a dark evergreen forest with Little Red Man on his back. The night sky overhead was brilliant with stars and the shimmering veils of the Northern Lights. Little Red Man looked over his shoulder toward where I stood, some feet away, and ordered, "Run with me!"

I explained that there was no way I could keep up.

He shook his head in mild disgust and replied, with some annoyance, "Very well."

I felt an ache and stretching in my legs, and I looked down to see them becoming those of a reindeer, my feet transforming into broad, spatulate hooves. My spine extended, forming a torso and then a second set of legs, and I became aware of the weight of the antlers now growing from my forehead. I wanted to speak, but all that came out was a throaty low bleat. And then we were off, bounding through the shin-deep snow across the tundra that bordered the taiga as I slipped away to sleep.

He has repeatedly asked me to ingest him, making clear that the amount can be miniscule, almost like a homeopathic dosage, the purpose of which is to help attune my energy or perhaps make me more open to his guidance. I'm not overly concerned about being poisoned by such a morsel, but I'll confess that I do want to approach such an act mindfully and respectfully.

Entheogens, those plants and fungi causing altered consciousness by virtue of their impact on the body's chemistry, have played a significant role in many shamanic cultures across the arc of time. Regrettably, "medicine plants" are used entirely too casually by would-be psychonauts who explore them recreationally and without going through the long process of building a relationship with the *vaet* or spirit of the plant or fungi. Since my very first encounter with mescaline in my late teens, I have honored the majesty and deep magic carried by entheogens and view them with reverence. Having often seen them abused, I regard them as the gift of the Gods, to be used only under very specific circumstances and always with respect. Like the San Pedro cactus that was one of my first spirit teachers and which I still grow, I am fortunate that dear Little Red Man is willing to teach me.

Building an alliance is the same with spirits as with humans. There must be mutual respect, give-and-take, even play. I still grow the San Pedro cactus given to me thirty-some years ago, and, while I no longer work in the Peruvian tradition, I treat this old friend with respect and care.

One dreary winter day, as I was watering my plants, the San Pedro sought my attention. "I want tassels," it communicated, showing me an image of the brightly colored woolen tassels often tied through the tips of llamas' ears.

I recalled that the descendants of the Incas believed that decorating their animals gave them pride and encouraged them to work more joyfully. I was more than happy to dig out a multicolored ball of yarn and spend a couple hours making red, yellow, and orange poufs to adorn my old friend. Periodically, all through the grey winter days, I could hear a contented giggle coming from the festive cactus. When I eventually had occasion to root cuttings and start a second pot of San Pedro, it, too, asked to be decorated.

It was quickly apparent that working with Little Red Man would also require cultivating a relationship with Reindeer. Long ago, I'd known a couple whose Victorian home was filled by all sorts of eccentric antiques and decorative objects, among which was a magnificent mount of the head and shoulders of a white caribou, the New World species of reindeer, crowned with magnificent antlers. Across the years, the memory of that noble creature stuck with me and, finally, I understood why.

As I worked with the spirit of Reindeer, he encouraged me to acquire one of his skins. After all, he and his kin had long provided hides to the peoples of the North. After looking at many pelts on-line, I was drawn to one – a thick silver and gray hide that had clearly come from a strong bull. Eric ordered it for my December birthday, and we eagerly awaited it.

When the parcel still had not arrived by the New Year, we joked that Reindeer was actually swimming the North Sea. Upon its arrival in mid-January, I welcomed Reindeer with recaning smoke, the song he'd taught me, and an offering of freshly harvested lichen.

"Antlers, too, please," he asked.

So, I began the search. Apart from antlers attached to the mounted heads of caribou taken by hunters, I learned that the majority of shed antlers were gathered and sold to China where the powder is prized as an aphrodisiac. I searched the internet and haunted Ebay until I noticed a pair of handsome antlers at auction. With Eric's help, we made the winning bid, and I was able to obtain them for a very reasonable price.

"I'll teach you about boundaries and self-defense," Reindeer advised me.

I welcomed his guidance, knowing that both were sadly lacking in my childhood instruction. The parcel, when it arrived, was huge.

"What y'all got coming from Norway in this big ol' box?" our rural postman asked.

I explained that they were reindeer antlers.

He shook his head in surprise, as he said, "Y'all sure do git some int'restin' mail."

True enough.

The fog of recovery was often pierced by powerful dreams and visions. Raven gave me books to study and assignments to familiarize myself with Norse lore and practical shamanic skills. Exercises were aimed at deepening my connection with the Elements, with the cycle of the year, with Day and Night. I needed to learn how to kindle Sacred Fire and practiced for hours with flint and a fire steel, knocking sparks into a bundle of soft, fluffy tinder – then, blowing gently until the flames caught. More difficult, still, is the fire bow, which is used to rapidly spin a central stick until friction generates sufficient heat to create an ember. We speak of Sacred Fire as our eldest Ancestor. Mastering the ability to create fire as the Ancients did so long ago is a reminder of the weighty spiritual legacy a traditional shaman carries. I already understood the core principle of shamanism – reciprocity – and worked at establishing new alliances with plants and animals held sacred in the Northern Traditions.

Having had little practice entering trance by means of a drum, I practiced finding and holding a rhythm I could "ride." I also loaded a shamanic drumming app onto my iPhone, in the event I wanted to journey but lacked a drum. I struggled to journey with the drum but soon discovered that I could use my phone to create evocative soundtracks for certain settings – combinations of nature sounds and ambient music that allowed me to shift from everyday consciousness and travel to other realms.

Raven wrote to ask me whether I had experimented with an old Norse practice called *utiseta* or "out sitting" (also referred to as "going under the cloak"). Practiced as a means of seeking wisdom and insight, *utiseta* was traditionally accomplished by spending the night out on a burial mound or other sacred place while wrapped in a cloak or blanket and makes use of a specific rhythmic breathing to enter an altered state of consciousness.

After practicing this special breathing for several months, I decided it was a good time to explore utiseta. *Throwing on my fur-trimmed cloak, I walked down to the still spot by the stream that we had dedicated to the Goddess Hel. I settled myself with my back against a huge tree and offered prayers to Freyja and the spirits of our land. As I stilled, I pulled the hood over my face and began the breathing pattern. With the first few extended breaths, I experienced some anxiety.* Would I get enough air? What if nothing happened? Would I actually manage to have a journey?

Somewhere along the way, pondering this, I slipped into another state and found myself standing in a long, narrow canoe-like boat, polling my way along the stream. It was night, and the stars twinkled through gaps in the trees arching over the stream. On either side of the boat were tall candle holders holding long, fat beeswax candles, their twin flames reflecting in brilliant ripples upon the surface of the stream as I moved quietly with the water's flow. There was little sound, apart from the occasional splash of a frog or fish and the sibilant song of the water against the boat's hull.

Where am I? *I wondered.* What is this place? Am I in Midgard or some other world?

As I progressed, the stream widened, and eventually it emptied into a small, shallow lake. At this point, I had lost all awareness of my physical body or the forest around me. I was wholly focused on my vision. I saw that a small island occupied the center of the lake, rising to a central hill cloaked in hardwoods. With a final push of my pole, I felt the prow of the boat grate on the gravel shore. Before me, a path led uphill through a gap in the trees. Leaving one candle burning so that I could find my way back to the boat, I took the other and climbed the hill, following the trail as it wound back and forth. Behind me, the newly waning moon rose against the late spring sky.

At the top of the hill, the trees along the path were hung with offerings of ribbons and bits of metal. I crested the rise and saw that the path led down into a small circular depression encircled by a tall stone wall. At the entry, I stepped through the gap and saw that, opposite me, across the bowl, was a large stone chair or throne set into the wall, covered by a peaked roof. By now the Moon was well up and its silvery light flooded into the clearing.

I went forward, and, as I approached the seat, She leaned out of the shadow, and chuckled. Her laugh was low and musical. "I've been waiting on you, you know."

Some part of me realized that hot tears were welling in my eyes. I had so hoped to see my Lady and, yet, had not dared to think that I might actually do so. I snuffed the remnant of the candle and stood with my head respectfully bowed before Her.

"Come here, Lítill Kǫttr." The phrase, meaning "Little Cat," was Her term of endearment for me. She held out Her hand and took mine, drawing me up into Her lap, cradling me against Her as a mother would her child. "You've had a hard time," She said tenderly. "I know all of this has been difficult."

Somehow I knew She meant my illnesses and the social isolation I'd dealt with over the past year, but also my shamanic studies.

"It was all to bring you to Me. I've watched you across the lifetimes, waiting for you."

I felt flooded by Her love, by Her belief in me, by Her compassion. Tears poured down my face.

Somewhere in the forest an owl called softly and Freyja smiled. "Do not lose hope, Lítill Kǫttr. You will remember this place and you will come back to sit with Me again."

She lowered me from Her lap and then gently traced Berkana, *rune of fertility and growth, on my forehead with Her fingertip. "Go now. The moon will light your way home."*

I bowed to Her, my cheeks damp, and turned to follow the trail back to the boat. I crossed the lake and began to pole my way back upstream. At this point, my trance was broken. I opened my cloak and sat for a while in the quiet dark, filled with wonder and gratitude.

Had I imagined the experience?

The runes, when I later checked them, said no.

My home, always cluttered with artwork and books, filled with altars and shrines as I cultivated devotional relationships with the Gods and spirits of the North. In the room that served as both guest space and study, a tall bookcase was given over shelf by shelf to images and objects honoring the deities and spirits I was coming to know and revere. I prayed to the Holy Powers, asking that They show what was expected of me. Occasionally, I was rewarded by Their guidance.

It has been said that ours is a tool-heavy tradition, a maker's tradition. Raven pointed out that we have no Elders to pass down sacred tools and, thus, must take responsibility for making our own. To create my own tools came naturally to me, and I found that I already owned some of the things I would come to need, such as my serpent staff. However, many of the tools were small, and I realized that I would need a chest for their storage.

I asked Eric if he would make me a *vaettir kista*, which is Old Norse for "spirit chest." We had several boards of beautiful Western Red Cedar left over from the building of my studio. I knew the strong, fragrant wood was lightweight and would protect my tools from insect damage. The chest was built to hold a removable tray and would close with an antique brass catch. Eric built and filled the golden brown, silky box with love.

We wanted to charge the chest to also act as a battery and protective ward. As it happened this year, the full Moon and summer solstice fell together through a rare celestial synchronicity for the first time since 1967. It felt important to honor my dual nature by capturing both moonlight and sunlight within the box as I awakened it. Somewhat after moonrise, but before Mani's silvery face appeared through the trees, Eric carried the box down to the upper *Ve*, where he lit the torches and blessed and charged the box with his intention before leaving me in the stillness of our standing stones. After thoroughly grounding and centering, I cleansed myself and the box with the spicy smoke of blessed rosemary. Then, I spoke my intentions. I honored the *landvættir* with bread and the Gods with offerings of beer.

With my shawl over my head, I sat down in the east-facing chair Eric had provided and took the box onto my lap. By this time, I could see moonlight peeking through the dark fretwork of the trees. I stroked the satin surface of the box, hallowing it with my hands, then, opened it and filled it with my breath, that it might know me. I re-latched the lid and began to caress it as I sang of the tiny seed that fell far away, that grew strong and tall over many years, that was harvested and prepared and assembled with love. I blessed the box with my tears: holy salt and water. Then, it was time to awaken it. I closed my eyes, beginning to tap and then to drum, exploring rhythms and pitches yielded by the top and sides and bottom, each piece of wood vibrating uniquely, coming alive.

Satisfied that the first part of the awakening was accomplished, I drew my shawl over my face and slowed my breathing. I didn't exactly expect to accomplish *utiseta*, but I wanted to be still and open. I prayed to Freyja, thanking Her for entering my life and asking Her to show me how I could best serve Her. For some time, I continued to just breathe, listening to the night noises, just being present…

Images passed through my mind like a slideshow until I stood before Freyja.

Her pale throat was adorned by a magnificently wrought gold and amber necklace. Her wheaten hair gleamed with red-gold highlights. The deep green gown She wore was embroidered with ripening grain. "Come with me, *Lítill Kǫttr*," She said. "There is something we need to take care of."

We were suddenly in a great and gleaming longhall, and She stood just behind me, with Her hands firmly on my shoulders. The wooden pillars supporting the dark smoky ceiling were richly carved and appeared to dance in the light cast by torches and the central fire. At the far end of the hall, on a raised dais and seated in a pair of carved and painted tall-backed chairs, were Odin and Frigga, surrounded by many Others I thought I recognized: one-handed Tyr, golden-haired Sif, even tricksome, flame-haired Loki. The hall had been busy, with much loud laughter and conversation, and as soon as we materialized, it grew quiet. I was aware of the All-Father's penetrating and intimidating presence.

Freyja, Mistress of Magic and of *Seidr*, Lady of Sessrúmnir, laid Her hand upon my shoulder and boldly met the All-Father's gaze. "This one is mine!" She declared firmly. "I *will* protect her, and woe be unto Anyone who harms her!"

Although I could clearly see Odin's displeasure that this daughter of the Vanir had beaten Him to His prize, my heart was flooded with love and relief. Then, She drew me aside to a table further down the hall and somewhat out of the way, where we could watch the goings-on. I noticed that She kept a hand on me at all times.

Mead was brought round. Upon the dais, a brawny fellow with a thick, rusty beard made a rude remark, His laugh booming out across the hall. Freyja leaned her head close to mine and reassured me, "That's Thor. No need to worry. To be honest, He's a bit of a blow-hard."

The feast began, and, then, I realized I was back in the everyday world, sitting in the *Ve* at TwoTrees with a magic box in my lap. Carefully moving on unsteady legs, I placed the box, with the lid open, on the stone altar, facing the rising full Moon. I hailed Mani and asked Him to pour His sweet pale light into her. Then, I opened the way, parting magical space, and came home.

The following day, the box sat open to the brilliant noon Sun of the summer solstice, so that Sunna could also bless my *vættir kista*.

I was filled with joy that I now unquestionably belonged to Freyja, although my near-death experience had certainly suggested it already. Of course, it made sense that I, who loved all things growing, who rescued cats, who was gifted in magic and struggled to value and love myself, should be claimed by the very Goddess who saved me at the brink of death. Initially, I wondered whether I had imagined my encounter, but Raven's subsequent independent divination affirmed that She had, indeed, established Her claim on me.

Eric commented on how She had kept a hand on me at all times. While I had initially thought She had done this to protect me, Eric felt that She was also probably giving me a boost of energy to allow me to sustain that visit.

In Freyja's honor, I now bear a tattoo of the rune *Fehu* overlaid on honeycomb and attended by a worker bee. I owe Her my life and will serve Her however long She desires.

Queen of Honey and Amber

Queen of honey and amber,
I knew you firstly from the bees' song:
The hum so soft, so filled with frith.
Each day I watched them come and go,
Focused, urgent, dedicated in their purpose.
Far and wide they soar,
Gathering the sweetness of the world.
Like You, they know the value
Of their gold and amber trove and guard it fiercely.
And when the battle is over,
They carry forth their valiant dead.
Like them, I serve my Queen.
The reward, both bold and sweet —
In sting, in honey, in sweet song of wings,
I know You, Vanadis.

Sixteen
BAGSHAGUI

This time of physical healing was also a time to take stock of the work to which I was being called. Many traditional shamans are specialists, and Raven and I undertook extensive divination to determine my strengths and which skill areas I was to undertake. We also discussed the ethics and boundaries of honorable shamanic practice, in many ways similar to those I'd followed as a massage therapist. If I was to continue to accept clients for healing and spiritual counseling, I wanted additional personal support and professional guidance.

I reached out to an old friend with a background in counseling who had worked in pastoral care at one of the local hospitals and for hospice. I knew Ken Bradstock to be inquisitive and broad-minded. He was a huge man with a twinkle in his eye and a booming laugh—blessed with the gift of making you feel that you were the most important person in the world. Every couple of weeks, Ken came over for tea and conversation: about faith, about shamanism, about counseling and pastoral work. When I asked him to mentor me and provide clinical supervision and guidance, he was delighted. For the next four years, until his untimely death, Ken was friend and teacher, father-figure, and fellow explorer. His departure left a huge bear-shaped hole in my heart.

While Ken knew a little about shamanism, I had lots of explaining to do. He asked respectful questions and listened with fascination as I shared some of my extraordinary experiences. In one of our first deep conversations, we explored how psychic aptitude and delusion can exist in continuity. I remarked that in the Northern Traditions, we joke that "psychically gifted" exists on a continuum with "bat-shit crazy."

Instead of recognizing that the range of human experience is very wide indeed, modern Western medicine is quick to pathologize those experiences that do not fit its narrow framing of "normal." In a society that marginalizes anyone who is different, it is not surprising that many people will seek out professional opportunities where their differences grant them the possibility of self-worth, if not rank or prominence. Some sensitive individuals find their way into New Age practices or those, like Core Shamanism, in which purchased training focuses on self-empowerment and self-healing. Others succumb to the isolation and confusion of having their atypical experiences written off as mental illness. And, scattered among the seekers are those who are genuinely called to this work in the midst of a culture that has no idea of what to do with us.

"I know how bizarre all this stuff sounds, Ken. I experience things that are certainly outside what most people would consider 'normal.'"

My friend studied me for a moment before offering important, non-judgmental feedback. "Do these experiences cause you distress?"

"Occasionally bewilderment, but not distress. This is my normal. I've had these experiences all my life."

He glanced at the art, comfortable furniture, and sleeping cats around us and grinned. "Looks like you're doing pretty well. You and Eric are happy, and you seem to be thriving in your life. That's really what we clinicians look for: Is the client in distress? Are they able to maintain meaningful relationships with others? Are they struggling in their lives?"

His booming laugh rang out. "Looks to me like you're thriving, Susannah. I don't think you need to worry that you're delusional."

Ken's helpful, practical criteria for considering this continuum has proved useful again and again when I've found myself with a client whose needs I was called to assess. Were the individual's experiences spiritual in nature? And when did I need to refer the client to someone with skills I lacked?

The following spring, I progressed to Level Two in my apprenticeship. Raven asked me to visit him so that he could work with me on his own sacred land. We decided that I would come for several days prior to Keepers Crossing – a gathering dedicated to Northern Shamanism – and stay over for the event. In July of 2016, Eric and I made the fourteen-hour drive to Massachusetts.

Over the years I have been blessed with a number of excellent teachers like Ken, all of whom helped to shape my expectations of the teacher-student relationship. In Raven's case, these expectations were also colored by his vibrant books. Our visit impressed on me that two people can use the same word and have it mean very different things to each of them. Say the word "cheese," and I think cheddar so sharp that it stings my tongue. Someone else may think of creamy, milky cottage cheese or of the plastic-wrapped, processed goo that is American cheese. While we might all claim to love cheese, we have in mind very different things. Even when we strive for clarity in communications and explicitness in our expectations, miscommunications can occur.

On Friday, I met other Northern practitioners – notably Galina Krasskova, polytheist scholar, and co-author with Raven of many books. Galina had a reputation for being stubborn and bluntly opinionated, but we somehow clicked quickly and comfortably. Knowing she was owned by Odin, I took the opportunity to talk with her about how the Old Man dogged me.

She cocked her head and looked at me in a way that reminded me of a wolf sizing up prey and remarked, "Yes, I imagine He would have. You have *power*, and power is useful.

He is nothing if not pragmatic."

Breaks between workshops offered the opportunity to get to know other individuals called to shamanic work in the Northern Traditions, and I was to encounter, for the first time, a community of individuals sharing many of the same challenges I had: non-traditionally gendered and neurodivergent in a variety of ways. The sense of belonging was intoxicating.

During the sweltering afternoons, various presenters spoke about the Beings described in Norse lore: the Aesir, the Vanir, and the Jötun or Giants—even of the Alfar or elves.

As I listened, I became aware of a stalwart Presence at my shoulder and a deep voice urged, "We want a place at the table. We want *you* to tell our story."

I realized that the Presence I sensed was that of Andvari, master smith of the Duergar, the Norse dwarves who are great magical craftsmen.

When I mentioned Andvari's demand to Raven, he nodded. "Sounds like you need to write a book."

Raven's divination indicated that I possessed an aptitude for trance work. He encouraged me to explore a technique described in the Norse lore often referred to as "oracular *seidhr*," but also called "spaework." In this process, the *Spaekona* (literally, Spywoman), enters a song-triggered trance, during which she becomes a medium for the spirits to speak through—a channel offering guidance or responding to questions. As a Pagan priestess, I had "carried" various Goddesses, and I figured this might be similar. For several months, I'd practiced using Raven's recording of a protective chant called a *vardlokkur* as a trance trigger but had never actually attempted to serve in this way.

After a single practice run, Raven surprised me by asking me to offer *spae* to the community on the final night of the gathering. Desiring to please my teacher and despite my misgivings, when Sunday evening rolled around I prepped as best I could. I settled myself into a chair at the center of the big labyrinth in Raven's back field with reindeer hides padding the grass at my feet. A group of strangers with profound personal questions gathered before me.

I had no clue whether anything would actually happen. *Go big or go home, right?*

As Raven sang the *vardlokkur*, I pulled my shawl over my face and prayerfully offered myself to the Holy Powers. My breathing deepened, my head dropped back, and opalescent light poured into me, displacing my conscious awareness.

At some point, I became aware of Raven singing the callback chant and of Eric taking my hands and calling my name. Like swimming up from deep water, I struggled back to ordinary consciousness. Eric helped me away from the group and brought me water, as well as a plate with roast chicken and strawberries.

I had apparently remained in trance about 30 minutes and had offered guidance to half-a-dozen querents. I had no recollection whatsoever of what I had said, although several people were to come up later to express their thanks for the guidance offered to them, remarking on how deeply moved they were by the experience.

In the weeks after we returned home, Eric, Kristy, and wise Ken patiently listened as I tried to sort out my concerns about my apprenticeship. I take oaths very seriously and had made a commitment to working with Raven. While I was having many new and exciting experiences in relationship with my teacher, I also craved active guidance as I navigated these strange waters. Instead, I found myself challenged to stand in the truth of my own perceptions and experiences, many of which differed from his. Would my allegiance be to my teacher, or to myself and the guidance of my own spirits? Would my apprenticeship meet my needs and those of my Holy Powers? Only time would tell.

Soon after returning home, Eric and I began cultivating our relationship with the Duergar or Dwarves, establishing a shrine to honor them and shamanically journeying together to Nidavellir, their underworld realm, where, to our surprise, we were greeted as kinsmen. Metalsmiths have always been regarded as magicians in shamanic cultures, and it fell to the two of us to explore that role in our community. Eric had a long-standing interest in blacksmithing, and I had made my living as a jeweler and sacred smith for decades.

In September, Kristy and I were scheduled to have a joint exhibition featuring my jewelry and her fiber art at a gallery in Salt Lake City. So, Eric and I traveled to Utah for a week-long visit combining vacation and business. The first days were devoted to exploring the wonders of Zion National Park, a place I visited long ago and longed to see again. Zion is a vast series of canyons, walls and mesas carved by water into the uplifted mass of the Colorado Plateau in southwestern Utah. Zion's clefts and canyons have provided a place of refuge for wildlife, as well as generations of human inhabitants and visitors. In the midst of harsh and arid desert, they offer scarce resources, shelter — and most precious of all — water.

Any landscape so long venerated develops strong vaettir; *in the case of Zion, the astonishing drama and beauty of the land somehow amplify the vibrant spirituality of the place. Sheer walls of red, pink, and cream sandstone soar thousands of feet above the narrow twisting course of the Virgin River, drawing the visitor's eyes heavenward to a sky of perfect turquoise. Brilliant sunlight paints the sculpted stone in ever-changing light and shadow, and everywhere*

one experiences the enduring power and importance of water.

Water has carved and still shapes the land itself. It dictates what areas can sustain life and what species will survive or thrive. Rain that falls far away, high on the Colorado Plateau, funnels ever downward into the surreal and luminous slot canyons that feed the narrow Virgin River or seep through porous layers of sandstone to emerge from exposed cliff faces as seeps and springs nurturing verdant oases whose lush greenness forms a striking contrast to the surrounding bare stone.

As we rode the visitor shuttle into the depths of the park on the first morning of our visit to Zion, a Paiute elder spoke (via a recording) about the significance of this land to his people and encouraged park visitors to be still and listen to the spirits of the place expressed through Nature. I wondered how many of my fellow visitors heard his message.

I felt drawn to return to a location referred to as the Weeping Wall. Over thirty years before, I had climbed this same steep slope with Kristy to do ceremony under a full Moon. At that time, I formed a link with the water spirit there. The simple gravel trail had been replaced by a paved one, and we climbed the series of switchbacks through atypically verdant drifts of plants whose very survival and lushness gave testimony to the feature we were seeking. A final bend in the trail revealed the vast belly of an arching, rusty sandstone cliff face, glazed and bejeweled by water and adorned in emerald drapery, including mosses and watercress. The water emerged from a permeable layer in the rock high on the cliff face to fall in a fine, sparkling shower across the wide arc. Rainbow shimmer hung in the moist air, accompanied by the delicate, echoing song of falling water.

As soon as I faced the cliff, I felt recognition and delight from the water spirit of the place. In the scale of time that carves the canyonlands, thirty years is but an instant. I hesitated, conscious of the other visitors behind me — torn between wanting to honor the magical being of this place and not wanting to create a spectacle. Almost overwhelmed by the energy of the place, I grounded and centered, asking what to do.

The call of the Sacred was strong; so, I bent to capture the blessed moisture in the cup of my hands. Softly, I began to sing.

The water spirit laughed in delight and stepped forward to smile at me from the glistening green of the cliff-face. For the briefest moment, I saw the world through her eyes and felt her delight that someone was acknowledging her presence. A soft, joyful chant emerged from my mouth – a song offered in praise of the miracle of water – and I knew I was echoing something offered by many before me, something that still resonated in the stone and water and wonder of that place.

As my everyday consciousness returned, I realized that some of the people around us were watching me with curiosity. I blew my breath over the water in my hands and released it to join the flow, thinking: This is what I was born to do – to bridge the boundary between Human and Spirit. Perhaps, through my actions, other humans may be reminded of a time when these Two were One.

Several days later, Eric, Kristy, and I arranged her beautiful fiber art, so full of magic, and my jewelry, just as magical, in a sunlit gallery in Salt Lake City. That evening, during the reception for the show's opening, I found myself in a conversation with two women who were discussing their distress over laws prohibiting transgender persons from using the restroom appropriate to their affirmed gender. For the first time in my life, I publically identified myself as an intersex person and spoke of my frustration with my own state's archaic, ignorant law. I didn't hesitate. I just finally spoke my truth.

Just prior to Yule, I undertook the making of a silver-mounted drinking horn as a gift for my husband. I had experimented with paper templates for the sterling silver mountings, exploring how to accommodate the curving, tapering horn. The silver mounting was to be decorated with a low relief of a Viking-style serpent and an inscription in runes around the silver rim: "He who drinks of me honors the Gods." Due to the advanced techniques involved, the project was very challenging, and I felt a great deal of uncertainty as to whether I could accomplish what I envisioned. I later wrote in *The Duergarbok*,

> Finally satisfied with the shape of my templates, I offered a prayer to the Duergar, petitioning them to guide me in my work. I wanted to use the same interlaced motif I had used on a cuff and buckle I'd previously made for Eric. As I began to work the silver, it quickly became apparent that I lacked chasing tools with the necessary curvature, so I broke away to create them, using some pieces of tool steel and my largest torch, and forged what I needed, a task I hadn't tackled for a number of years.
>
> The next day, with my energy clearer and more focused than it had been for some time, I continued with the chasing of the beast decorating the rim of Eric's horn. Much to my distress, the effect was very rough, and I realized I had to come up with a way to salvage the piece or else order more silver and explain to my Beloved why his gift was late. With nothing to lose, I decided to see whether I could use a combination of chasing and repoussé to salvage the project. I'd never attempted "full on"' repoussé before, and it is a tedious and time-consuming technique, but, as I worked, I became more optimistic that the piece might turn out. After all, all I could do was to proceed, and, if it didn't work out, scrap it and start over.
>
> Most of the third day's work was spent completing the relief, annealing the silver, and then slowly and painstakingly bending and fitting the band until the ends lined up. I sang as I worked,

something I often do, and felt centered and energized. Once this was done, I soldered the joint and continued with the fitting, made the gallery wire overlay and soldered that in place and prepared to secure the rim to the horn. I couldn't recall when I'd last spent seven straight hours in the shop, but it was good to know I could still do it!

Then, I hit the proverbial brick wall. Due to the tapered shape of the horn, I couldn't for the life of me reason out how to secure the rim in place. In a moment of despair, I offered a heart-felt prayer to the Duergar, pledging that henceforth I would give my utmost effort to every creative task I undertook for the remainder of this lifetime, if they would only show me how to complete the horn. Exhausted and near to tears, I closed down the shop, locked up and went back to the house.

Perhaps, the Duergar decided to be helpful or else took pity on my clumsiness, but when I returned to my bench the following morning, I could see clearly the steps necessary to complete the horn! My oath was not lightly made, and I continue to strive to fulfill it in every creative project I undertake.

Galina's on-line classes fed my hunger for a more scholarly approach, and our correspondence and phone conversations offered new knowledge and encouraged my skills. Thanks to my prior shamanic work, I moved through the Guild syllabus quickly and soon was approaching my initiation, the transformative ritual that imparts mysteries and tests one's power and alliances with the spirits. Such a rite would mark my ability to work independently as a shaman in the Northern Traditions. However, as events unfolded, this elevation was not to take place as I had dreamed, with rich ceremony and celebration, witnessed by friends, family, and colleagues.

In 2017, toward the end of May, Galina broke completely with Raven, an abrupt and remarkable end to a long-term collegial relationship. At the heart of the schism was Galina's intense focus on piety and a style of working diametrically opposed to Raven's. In essence, his emphasis was on usefulness to the community while hers was on spiritual devotion. I saw and experienced the value of both paths and struggled to understand the conflict.

My distress and sadness were profound, and I was deeply uncertain of how to proceed. I spoke at length with both parties about the conflict and my concerns, bridging between my Elders as I had once been the bridge between my quarreling parents. This concept of serving as a bridge, which had expressed itself in many ways throughout my life, has integral roots in my identity as one who is simultaneously both male and female, one capable of holding different perspectives simultaneously.

Looking for a host site other than Raven's farm, I researched more centrally located options for Keepers Crossing and rented an old farmhouse in Central Pennsylvania for the long weekend, filling in for Galina and teaching the morning workshops while Raven taught the afternoon slots. Once again, I offered a *spae* ceremony for those attending. Throughout the event I remained unsure as to whether or not I would continue as Raven's apprentice and remain a member of the Guild. Even my divination had given ambiguous advice.

My own work was being increasingly guided by older Mongolian and Siberian spirits, and I had begun to think in terms of the Northern Traditions (plural and collective) rather than the Northern Tradition (singular and Norse). Most daunting of all, Freyja had informed me that the Guild schism was both ordeal and initiation for me. As the event wound down, Raven and I sequestered ourselves and entered into an intense discussion.

"What do you want?" he finally asked.

"Freyja says it's time for you to embrace me as a colleague," I responded.

We turned to the runes for guidance: the divination confirmed that I was to be elevated from apprentice to shaman—Level Four—and would now continue my studies independently, establishing my own practice and training my own apprentices. I was now to be *bagshagui*, spirit-taught.

I was presented with a ceremonial headpiece secretly made for me by Raven and my fellow apprentices, but learned the hard truth of Freyja's determination that I follow an independent path. I found that I could not wear the headpiece. Puzzled, I prayed and asked for clarification.

"Find your own way," Freyja directed. "Others may receive their tools as gifts, but you must make yours, because only you can sense what will be right for you."

This was hard to hear—gifts carry intention and goodwill, as well as a special type of luck called *hamingja*, a luck I would not have the benefit of with self-made tools and regalia. I felt adrift and quite alone.

Each day, I prayed for guidance and one evening was rewarded when a stout, dark-haired Duerg appeared at the foot of my bed.

"You promised to tell our story," he reminded me firmly.

Determined to respond to Andvari's prompting, I began to write of my own experiences as a sacred maker and smith. The call for submissions for *The Duergarbok* went out and contributions started to roll in. Both Raven and Galina graciously made material available, and I drew on my own extensive notes, knowing that however I wrote this book, there would be traditionalists who would find fault, as well as readers who would consider my accounts the product of fantasy or delusion.

So be it.

My task was to do my best to produce what had previously not existed: a book gathering together accounts of human interactions with these Beings of legend in our modern world.

After all, I had given over my life to the service of Gods and spirits whose very existence might be questioned by many, having my very life saved by One. Where in the twenty-first century is a person to find guidance for such a calling? Or, perhaps, mine was a road less taken, a journey to be negotiated by honoring my instincts and trusting Higher Guidance.

Bagshagui.

I was on my own, no longer accompanied by human guides, but in the company of a vast circle of spirit teachers.

Season Four

Autumn, Harvest

Astringent walnuts and final, bursting muscadines
Fuel the hunger to hunt, to gather, to couple.
Wood smoke hangs in the October's air,
Signaling a welcomed homecoming
And the rush of preparation as summer slips away.
We feast on late fallen apples mellowed by the frost and
Honeyed bread warm from the oven,
Washed down with the last mead of summer.
One red leaf tumbles, as slanted sunlight
Illuminates golden poplars and garnet sourwoods.
Above the neighbor's vacant cornfield
An exultant hawk cries upon the late wind.
Musky mushrooms perfume the woodlands
Sharp with the tang of ripening hickory nuts and
Fat, glossy acorns, yeasty and fulsome.
As night falls, Orion rises like a promise kept,
While beneath the Hunter's Moon
Ghostly beeches gleam and owls inquire.
Urgent spirits have me standing,
Feet planted in both worlds
As the Dead dance 'round me in their wistful cotillion.
Strange renewal in this season of endings:
Desire, oh sweet Desire, sharp as the hunter's arrow.

Seventeen
SPIRITS, GHOSTS, AND WISE ANCESTORS

My place in the Northern Tradition community was a curious one. While I was no longer a shamanic apprentice, I remained a Guild member. There was no precedent I could turn to for guidance about my role and responsibilities. So, as an independent practitioner, I continued to build alliances, refine my tools, and hone my skills.

I was finding Soul Map readings to be especially helpful in work with my clients. Used by Northern Tradition shamans and shamanic practitioners for exploring the elements of the human soul, the system is described at length by Raven Kaldera in his book, *Wyrdwalkers: Techniques of Northern Tradition Shamanism*. With seventeen graphic symbols paired with a complex divinatory process, the Soul Map can offer remarkably accurate insights into a client's strengths, weaknesses, and blockages as well as the role that the Gods, Ancestors, and spirits play in the individual's life. During the early months of my studies with Raven, I had created a painted Map. While it worked adequately for my purposes as a student apprentice, the Duergar would remind me of my pledge to strive for excellence. This would challenge my focus and my needlework skills as nothing else had. I described that experience in *The Duergarbok*:

> I found myself increasingly aware of small faults in the artwork, of a lack of connectivity that had nothing to do with lack of signal clarity on my part. "You can do better," the Duergar whispered. "You know it isn't right." Was the prob-

lem the symbols I'd used, my materials, my workmanship? I sat with the Soul Map on my lap, inviting guidance.

"You wouldn't make a sword out of copper, would you?"

I thought about the power in my teacher's Soul Map, exquisitely embroidered on heirloom linen, and of the inherent connection between any form of fiber work and the *Wyrd*, the threads of causality spun and held and severed by the Norns. In a conversation about how different forms of fiber-work hold energy, he'd commented that chain stitch seemed to carry magic and intention particularly well. Perhaps, it was how thread carries intent, or the three-dimensional quality of embroidery, or even the state of mind one enters into while doing this craft. But it was clear that I, too, must undertake to embroider my own Soul Map.

Having made this decision, I began by making an offering to the Duergar and asking them to guide me in my work, that it might embody the skill and excellence I so honored in them. Over the next several weeks, I journeyed to gather clear images that might represent for me the seventeen symbols representing the Soul Map Elements. Next, I studied a wide selection of historical designs in my hunt for those that would comprise a suitable border and began a series of sketches made to scale, to explore and adjust how the components related visually and energetically. Satisfied, I made a master pattern using a black micro pen and colored pencils, their colors based on those available in the palette of natural dyes available to the Norse and Anglo-Saxons. After much searching, I settled on a snowy midweight Irish heirloom linen. I hand-washed it and whipped the edge so the fabric would not fray and then meticulously transferred my design using an archival marker and lightbox. I'd managed to find six-strand cotton floss to match my color palette, and decided to work in single and double strands to maximize my control and detail.

For the next four months, I worked for six to eight hours every day. I washed my hands, threaded my tiny English needle, said a prayer, and stitched. First, the Element symbols, each completed in the appropriate sequence. I shaded and painted with thread until the "Done!" light came on in my head, then moved on to the next one. Next, I turned to the ornamental squares anchoring the corners and middles of the borders. And finally, the intricate interlacing beasts, their elongated legs, necks and tails intertwining. Many times I sewed for some time, only to be told to pick the work out and start over. And, that's what I did. When the embroidery was done and the finished piece gently washed again, I carefully backed it with dark-blue hand-dyed cotton. It felt alive, sentient, like no other thing I'd ever made.

Since then, I've done Soul Map readings for many clients and friends using this tool, and the level of clarity and insight I obtain through it never ceases to amaze me. And thus, the Duergar lesson: the clarity of intent, care, focus, skill, and meticulous effort invested in a sacred tool absolutely determines that tool's magic and power.

Traditional spirit alliances are always reciprocal and the product of sustained and mutually respectful interaction. The idea of working with animal spirits has entered popular culture through pseudo-shamanic writers like Carlos Castenada, to the extent that there are dozens of books and workshops and websites dedicated to "Finding Your Power Animal." This is so common that there are running jokes about white male spiritual seekers always imagining themselves to be allied with large carnivores such a Bear, Panther, or Wolf as a reflection of their need to feel powerful.

Among the peoples of the North, it is common for a shaman to seek alliances with spirits that fly, run, swim, and burrow, so that they might readily move through the various worlds. Several allies assist me in Earth work and Owl assists me for Air work. Imagining a watery creature of the North, I had assumed I might eventually work with Salmon or Seal, but a surprise awaited me.

Seated on a large rock beside the cold, splashing waters of Town Fork Creek, I dropped into my breath and opened my awareness, sinking into dark, cold depths, only to feel an ancient consciousness brush mine: Sturgeon! One of the eldest of bony fishes, dating back to the Triassic Period, Sturgeon was not a fish I would have sought out in hope of an alliance. I could see him, enormous and lying very still on the muddy floor of a cold, very deep lake, moving just enough to oxygenate his gills. His skin was scarred and his eyes clouded with age. I realized he was a Grandfather fish spirit, like Lady Mugwort is a Grandmother plant spirit. Grandfather Sturgeon showed me his life, from egg to fry to fingerling, his slow growth over the long arc of years.

Sturgeons feed in the murk of lake and river bottoms, using sensitive barbels located beneath a nose-like rostrum to detect mollusks and shellfish hiding in the mud. This Ancient One advised: "You need to learn discernment, child. Trust what you feel, not what you see. The world can be a cold, dark place, but with care, you can find your way. My task is to teach you patience," he told me. "You humans are so hasty and shortsighted, and you only see the world in terms of yourselves."

This important lesson was one I was to be taught in another, more painful way.

Today, I walked the hillside below the house to look for a tree willing to be harvested to serve as a God pole for Freyr. I took a few moments to ground and center, but failed to put up any shields — something I've never felt the need to do on our land. Then, I spoke to the spirits of the land and asked their help in finding a likely tree.

I could feel some likely trees below and to the west of me, and I made my way toward them. The forest energy grew more and more resistant, somehow thicker and darker. In the final buffer wall of great pines, I spotted an adolescent hickory about 9 inches in diameter. I scanned the trunk and realized there was a large bird's nest in the crown, perhaps that of an owl. Reluctant to cut this tree, I quickly noted another slightly smaller tree about ten feet further on.

Approaching the smaller tree, I encountered a barrier of thick catbrier vines blocking my path. I spoke to Catbrier, experiencing her as protective and defensive. Thinking the issue was her perception that I was somehow a threat, I reassured her I meant her no harm. I used my walking stick to make an opening by carefully lifting the exceedingly thorny vines aside and carefully stepped through. I had just begun to connect with the vaet of the hickory when I felt white-hot pain in my left hand and again on the back of my right arm. I caught a quick glimpse of a wasp nest covered with very angry black wasps in the undergrowth next to me. I abandoned my walking stick and took off running as if all the hounds of Hel were after me. Miraculously, I received only the two stings.

I immediately realized that I'd been so focused on getting to that hickory and trying to reassure Catbrier of my benign intent that I failed to understand that she was actually trying to alert me to danger, to communicate that it was not safe for me to pass. Her twining stems extended to the nearby dogwood where the wasps had built *their nest, and when I shifted them, I jostled the nest and the wasps did what threatened wasps do: defended their home.*

It's my tendency to wander about when in the woods — a product of how strongly I feel and hear the spirits of the plants, animals, and stones and how readily I slip into the Between in the forest. This lesson, a painful one, also reminded me that I've always experienced a sense of utter safety and impunity in the woods since my childhood in the Uwharrie hills. I was reminded that Nature is not always pretty and benevolent and that as I journey more deeply into this life of service, I must be more vigilant and more mindful.

One of the issues I found myself confronting was the question of whether to charge for my services. In many Indigenous cultures, the shaman or healer is valued as a community resource and thus supported by the tribe who provide for their needs. In such cultures, it is the custom to bring a gift when seeking help or guidance, but practitioners rarely require payment. The idea that practitioners should not charge for their services has somehow made its way through New Age beliefs into modern society, and so whether to require payment has become a point of contention. Although people never question paying for bodywork or housekeeping or therapy, for whatever reason, they hold the belief that charging for ceremonies or shamanic work is "unspiritual."

While there is much agreement about the need for ordained professional clergy and skilled healers among various Pagan and Heathen denominations, there seems to be little willingness to fund such professionals or provide for their needs. Some of my colleagues work on a "by donation" basis, and I am acutely aware that many clients possess limited resources. At the same time, experience has taught me that people tend to value more what they have paid or bartered for. Having been conditioned to be helpful and accommodating as a child, I habitually undervalue myself and my work, an issue for which Freyja took me to task. Among Her many other attributes, She is known for teaching self-worth and healthy boundaries.

"Lady," I prayed. "What should I do about charging for my services? You directed me to ask compensation for my *spae* work. What about divination and healing?"

Her response was firm. "Remember that *Gebo*, Sacred Exchange, is at the heart of respect and worthiness. Your life is given over to Holy Work, and you always strive to give your best. Know, therefore, that you are deserving of recompense and should be compensated for your skill, for your wisdom, and for the supplies and materials needed in your work. You have no tribe to feed you but must earn your bread and meat like others in this time and culture. Of course, it is right to accommodate those of limited means, but even they benefit from *Gebo*."

Eventually deciding on what felt to be reasonable fees for my services, I also concluded that I would charge a moderate fee for the public classes and workshops I had begun to offer, but also that I would not participate in the "Pay to Learn" culture established by Core Shamanism. When the time came for me to accept my own apprentices, I would not charge them for their training.

My reputation for skilled geomancy – the art of optimizing the health of the land – led to my being called in to assess a piece of property in an affluent older neighborhood in town. This was to prove to be one of the more remarkable projects I have undertaken. The owners had been experiencing an unusual amount of ill will and belligerence from a neighbor and felt something was "off." When walking the property I experienced the distinct sense that it held a history of trauma. A survey map of the property indicated an old well was located on the boundary with the problem neighbor. Research revealed that the neighborhood had originally been made up of family farms, bought up by an aggressive developer in the 1920s. I journeyed for more insight, traveling back through time to witness someone cruelly and maliciously throwing a farmer's much-loved cat into the well to starve. The brutal act generated a great deal of toxic energy, populating the well with a very angry cat ghost.

With Eric's assistance, the help of my spirits, and protection from Freyja and Mother Jaguar, I was able to help the angry feline spirit to transition. Offerings were made and magical wards were placed to deflect negative energy from the client's property, profoundly transforming the energy there. In a short time, the problem neighbor sold his home to a friendly family, and the blocked and unhealthy areas of my client's lot began to heal. Later, the landowner was to share with me many occasions when visitors remarked on how transformed the property felt.

The impact of trauma lingers, whether in people or in places. That summer, Eric and I drove to southwest Georgia to pick up an anvil he was purchasing, unaware that our route would pass near the infamous Andersonville Prison Camp, used to hold Union prisoners at the end of the Civil War. Heading south from Atlanta, I noted how unwell the countryside felt, all scrub pine and kudzu barrens. Abruptly, I found myself swarmed by the ghosts of men who had suffered and died in that wretched hell-hole, boys begging for water, food, their mothers, their sweethearts. Gasping, I quickly shielded myself in self-protection, explaining to Eric what I'd just experienced. We pulled over to look at a map and realized how near we were. It was apparent that the terrible miasma generated by such a place stretched out for miles—and as an unwitting sensitive, I had blundered right into it.

I have long felt drawn toward battlefield healing, often sensing such spots without being told of them. During the Civil War, two of my own great-great-grandfathers had spent time in the Union prison camp at Elmira, New York, so it was little surprise to me that these wretched Dead would reach out to me. This experience was to initiate for me deeper studies of family genealogy and ancestral healing. The latter would become an important part of my emerging practice.

Over the previous decade of my journey, I had shifted from being a massage therapist and sacred smith, engaged in a deeply spiritual relationship with my husband and our land, to being a full-time spirit worker. I gradually regained my health, along with a new sense of focus. As I explored this new identity, many spirits shared their sacred songs with me, and my rapport with Lady Freyja deepened. My first year as an independent practitioner proved rich and productive.

Freyja is associated with cats and amber and if She had Her way, I'd rescue ALL the cats and buy ALL the amber. Instead, we negotiate.

"Lady," I ask Her, "if You really want that amber, would You please provide the means?"

Today, She pokes me and tells me to go look on a particular website She likes. She whispers,"There's amber..."

I sigh and do as She asks.

"Not that one...nor that one..."

This pattern goes on through several pages of options.

A particularly nice necklace from Sweden pops up marked half off, and it's a steal. She nudges. "How about splitting the cost?"

I know when I've been played.

In Norse lore, Freyja is considered the Queen of *Seidr*, the Norse name for magical and shamanic practices, including spell-work, sexual magic, and *spae* or visionary mediumship. She explained that the *spae* protocol Raven had taught me was adequate for an apprentice just learning but that I now needed greater protection. In addition, She taught me a new *vardlokkur* or spell song which I was to sing to induce my own trance. She informed me that, as there must be Sacred Reciprocity, querents must bring something to offer in compensation for the service I would offer. At that summer's Northern Shamanism gathering, against some push-back from Raven about the new *vardlokkur*, I put this new protocol to the test and found it much easier to enter the *spae* trance.

> *Open the way, that my spirit may pass*
> *Over the mountains and under the seas.*
> *Open the way that my soul may go faring*
> *Through all the Nine Worlds that encircle the Tree.*

At the same time, I was working on my own personal traumas. Although I had been in therapy in the past, I decided it was time to take a different approach with my healing. I sought out a local practitioner of somatic therapy and attachment theory. Kirtan and I met many years before when I worked at Wellsprings, where we had both studied Peruvian Shamanism with the same teacher. We related well then, and I felt instinctively she would be a good fit as a therapist. Ken Bradstock also continued to offer personal encouragement and professional support. This personal work, in addition to the healthy perspectives offered by friends and advisors, grounded me ever more strongly in my own practice.

I made the powerful decision to free myself from societal programming about how I should dress or look. I had never really felt comfortable dressing in women's clothing and had come to wear my iron-gray hair buzzed short. With Eric's support, I began to be more open about being intersex.

The whole point of my therapy was to mobilize and release the accumulated traumas I had sequestered within me. I prayed to Freyja, to my Ancestors, and to the primary allies who had become such a significant part of my life and work. That night, in a dream, Reindeer came to me and showed me a vision. In it, I lay on my back on the floor with his hide beneath me, a shawl over me like a shroud, candles at the ends of my outstretched arms and Reindeer's antlers laid over my legs like a protective basket or sleigh.

He instructed, "Rest upon my back, and my antlers and sharp hooves will keep you safe."

After supper the following evening, I asked Eric for his help. I cleansed myself and made offerings and prayed at my altars. Freyja told me to wear Her amber. I lit charcoal and set some incense smoldering, honoring the powers of each direction with *galdr* to aid in my release. Then, I sang to call upon my Holy Powers. Spreading Reindeer's hide on the floor, I lay down. Eric arranged the shawl over my face and body with the antlers embracing my legs. He lit the candles and turned off the lights. Then, he began to drum over my torso at the tempo I'd taught him, softly at first, then increasingly loudly.

I began by softly toning the rune *Laguz*, embodying flow, with LA on the inhale and GUZ on the exhale, hoping to open myself so that the blocked energy in me could move. Dropping into trance, I found myself lying on the back of a huge white reindeer, racing through the snow. I felt utterly safe and secure as I rocked under a vast arctic night sky where the aurora danced and flickered, veiling crystalline stars against vast blackness. Deep snow stretched out from us and I could see, out of the corner of my eye, the dark, spiky tree-line to our far left.

The night was sharply cold and the air sweet and clean, the snow crunching with each of Reindeer's steps, our breath emerging as vapor. Curiously, although I experienced myself as wearing the clothing I had on in the consensual reality (jeans and a knit shirt), I was not cold. I glanced to either side and saw that we were accompanied by two ravens whom I immediately knew to be Huginn (Thought) and Muninn (Memory). Ahead of us flew Owl, scouting the way. Although I faithfully honor my allies and experience their presence from time to time, the promptness and concreteness (for lack of a better term) of their presence in this working was very affirming.

Tears came almost immediately: I was deeply moved by the beauty of the setting, the glorious swirling aurora above, the sense of safety I felt with Reindeer. I began to chant in a language that seemed familiar but which I could not identify, a syllable with each drum strike, building the emotional tide by tensing and relaxing my muscles.

I thought of my brother and all the pain and anger our relationship has engendered. I allowed my grief for my late parents to surface, my bewilderment over all the curious complexities of our relationships. I experienced myself then as the small boy I never got to be and wept for that child. I could feel the energy swelling within me and knew I needed to vent it, but for some time could not bring myself to make any sound.

Then, I thought about how this was part of how I was stuck in the frozen state in the first place, recalling all the times I was told to be brave, to be stoic, and not to cry. So, I forced myself to make sound. It emerged as a raw, guttural howling that eventually shifted into wracking sobs. I wept until I could weep no more and signaled Eric to wind down the drumming. He came and knelt beside me, and, when I was able, I reached out to take his hand.

Powerful stuff.

My therapist encouraged me to connect locally with others who shared my values, and I reached out to Sydney Hughes-McGee, a bodyworker and organizer of Winston Salem's 18 Springs Community Healing Center. The 18 Springs community is progressive and dynamic, with a strong emphasis on social justice, which was a good fit for me.

Many cultures associate autumn with the Dead — the Celtic Samhain and Hispanic celebration of Día de los Muertos being well known examples. I set aside October as a time to commit myself even more deeply to honoring my People. I worked on my genealogy, did ceremonies, journeyed to heal family rifts and traumas, and found myself engaged even more passionately in relationship with my forebears. Ancestor veneration is a significant and deeply personal part of Northern spiritual traditions. As an Animist who views everything as enspirited, I am often conscious of the presence of my Dead around me. Their very struggles and journeys are embedded in my DNA, shaping me in a variety of ways. I am the product of millions of years of human resourcefulness, courage, and adaptation, and I have profound gratitude for my Ancestors.

Altar work offers a deeply meaningful way to engage with one's forebears. In the room where most of my altars and shrines are located, I set aside a shelf just for my Ancestors, adorning it with pictures of my Dead and small objects that were theirs or gifts from them: a locket of my mother's silver hair, my father's harmonica, a grandmother's mosaic brooch, a tiny tin box of amalgam from my grandfather's dental practice. This altar also holds tokens that remind me of Ancestors of Choice, those who, although not blood kin, have had a profound positive impact on my life. At various times of the year, I add flowers, candles, food, and drink—typically items especially enjoyed by my Dead during their lives.

I often sit before this shrine and talk with my Dead or sing the songs that came down in my family. I ask them for guidance and support and express my gratitude for the life they have made possible. Was my family perfect? No, because people are complicated and life can be traumatic. *As you heal, we heal*, they remind me. Baptist Ancestors active in the Temperance Movement informed me that they weren't happy with the offering of whisky I'd been making, and would I please instead offer them a glass of fresh water in the future. My mother's folk, some of whom had been moonshiners, were happy to have the booze on their side.

We walk in the steps of our Ancestors:
They live in the songs we sing.
We honor their courage, for life was hard,
So let our praises ring —
Hail, hail the Ancestors who lived that we might, too.
Mother's blood and Father's blood has now found life in you.
Hail, hail the Ancestors who live in us this day,
And so we sing to honor them, who help us find our way.
And so we sing to honor them, who help us find the way!

Eighteen
A COAT AND A DRUM

In every culture embracing shamanism, the practitioner accumulates, whether by purchasing, making, or inheriting, ritual tools and ceremonial clothing, the function of which is to enhance their power and effectiveness. We don't know what Northern ancestral shamans would have worn, but we can take our cues from the Mongolian and Trans-Siberian cultures who are our cousins and who have managed to maintain intact cultural practices.

In these Northern Traditions, the shaman's coat is the badge that signifies that one has given one's life in service to the Gods and spirits. Although the construction and materials may vary significantly from one tradition or tribe to another, shamans' coats have in common their function: to act as energetic batteries for the shaman to draw upon and as spiritual armor to protect the practitioner from harmful energies and spirits. In Mongolia, most shamans' coats are cut in the style of the *deel*, a loose, caftan-like garment with overlapping front panels, most often made of heavy silk brocade. Given that silk is an excellent insulator, this makes perfect sense. As one moves northward, the nomadic reindeer herders are more likely to use leather and fur. Not only are these materials warmer, but they are also more readily available. Regardless of the foundation material, these ritual garments all seem to be adorned with a collection of objects having significance for the wearer and can be extremely heavy.

Historically, shamans' coats were made by specific shamans who specialized in their creation, with the recipient adding talismans, charms, and power objects over time. Other shamans, referred to as whitesmiths (in contrast to blacksmiths) specialize in the making of the talismans and the bells, tiny tools, and weapons often added to the coats. It is common for the family of the candidate to commission the coat to be sewn by particular seamstresses according to directions given in dreams, through divination, or as guided by the candidate's teacher.

In a process that took months, I designed and made my own coat. After collecting an extensive archive of pictures of shamanic regalia, I began a series of journeys, asking my patron Deities and ally spirits what would please Them. The journey work I undertook to seek guidance engaged me with spirits strongly associated with the shamanic traditions of Northern Eurasia, my dear Little Red Man, the North Wind, Owl, Horse, and Reindeer. The latter was a creature deeply important to these cultures and perhaps the first animal to have been domesticated by our Ancestors. While silk would have been far easier to sew, I was instructed that my coat would need to be made of leather.

I began to search for a source for reindeer leather but found it impossible to order, so I turned to buttery deerskins from the red deer of New Zealand, a closely related species. The design was to have layers of leather feathers arranged like a cape over the upper body in homage to Owl and trailing fringes. I ordered hand-woven trim from Uzbekistan in the golds, greens, and browns I associate with the Vanir I serve and put out a call for charms to represent my spirits and allies.

Friends and colleagues sent me a wide assortment of items bearing their good wishes and shared luck. Some I was guided to add to the coat; others were set aside for future uses or passed on to colleagues. To help with the protective aspect of the coat, I made numerous small bronze shamanic mirrors called *tolis* to deflect harmful spirits. I also created spirit traps, small brass hexagons pierced with an intricate design to capture attacking hostile spirits. From copper and bronze, I fabricated miniature tools and weapons that I suspended from the coat's many fringes: bows and arrows, a tiny boat, a ladder, a sword, all for use in other realms. Freyja explained to me that iridescent mother-of-pearl buttons would also deflect harmful spirits, so I embellished the coat with dozens. Bells are also common in a variety of shamanic cultures. In addition to random bells that were gifted to me out of the blue, I ordered a hundred small brass "Tiger" bells, only to discover once I'd sewn them to the coat that they chimed at the same pitch as my constant tinnitus.

"No way you'll ever sneak up on any spirits in that coat," Eric observed, trying not to laugh.

As I worked, I found myself thinking about all the time and care I have put into creating my shamanic tools and regalia. I have come to believe that the act of creation is a means of honoring the Gods. What will become of these things when I am gone? Some will pass to my own apprentices; others will be ritually burned.

My coat has grown quite heavy. I subjectively estimated its weight at 25–30 pounds; however, when I donned it and stepped on the scales, we were surprised to find it only added 8 pounds! I've attached a pair of ravens carved from glossy black buffalo horn to the coat's shoulders in honor of Odin's Huginn and Muninn. I added tiny brass bee charms and invited friends and colleagues to contribute small items bearing their good wishes and prayers for me.

Most remarkably, while perusing Etsy one day, I came across a remarkable conch shell disc carved with a jaguar in ancient Meso-American style. Although not a Northern creature, Jaguar was my first ally and strongest protector. Perfect for guarding my back!

As I sewed on a charm for Sleipnir, Odin's eight-legged steed,
the coat informed me it wanted horsehair tassels. So back I went to
Etsy, source for all sorts of shamanically useful supplies, to purchase
black horsehair and brass cones. Once these arrived, I went to work,
and soon the already very fringy coat bore dozens of flowing horse-
hair tassels.

I admired this remarkable garment and gave thanks for my
spirits' guidance in its making. It's strongly enspirited, both through
my prayers and intent as I made it, as well as through all the things
added to it.

"My name is Hestr," it said — Horse.

On the final day of April, the time came to formally hallow
my coat. I thought about how this bitter-sweet event was the
only real initiation in the Northern Traditions I would have.
Although Raven had previously spoken of an initiation ceremony for me at TwoTrees, Freyja advised that it was not to be.
I would have no supporting community to stand witness and
lend encouragement, no Elders present to do divination on
my behalf, no community to feast and celebrate with me. This
realization filled me with deep sadness.

After Eric and I had supper, I gathered our offerings:
ginger liqueur and an apple for Freyr and Freyja, whiskey
and cakes and a beeswax candle. In the golden light of early
evening, Eric recaned me with fragrant rosemary smoke, and,
then, I recaned the coat as he held it for me.

I slipped it on, acutely aware of the significance of what we
were about to do.

Holy Powers, Blessed Ancestors —
Bless me, your child.

Let me see and appreciate the wonders of the world around me.
Help me to sink my roots deeply into Mother Earth
And raise my branches joyfully to Father Sky.
Help me to be discerning, to trust my gut, to speak my Truth.
Grant me the strength and courage to do the work of healing
So that I may fulfill all I am called to be.

For the first time, I experienced a sense of the coat as a warm, living presence, fragrant and supple. I blessed the deer who had given their skins for its making, the fox and snake bones, buttons and bells and charms, many gifted with warm good will from those dear to me.

With Eric carrying the offerings, his silver-mounted drinking horn, and my drum, I took up my staff and began my journey. I went first to the bee yard to hail the Little Sisters and then to Freyr's cherry tree where we often leave offerings before progressing to the upper *Ve*. The golden light of late evening streamed through the woods and birdsong surrounded us. I placed the apple and a cake in the offering plate on the *hörgr* as Eric transferred the ginger liquor I had made to the horn.

Upon the horn's silver rim, a runic inscription gleamed: "He who drinks of me honors the Gods." I saluted the Holy Powers and took a sip before offering it to Eric so he could do the same. I hailed Freyr and made *blót*, the Norse term for an offering. I poured out the golden liquor to My Lady. Taking up my drum, I sang to call power and my allies. I could feel the presence of my Ancestors, actual and spiritual, gathered in sacred witness.

From there, we made our way down the trail and across to the grotto we had dedicated to the Duergar. There, I hailed our Dwarven kinsmen and offered cake and whisky, expressing my thanks for their instruction and for the extra energy they had tucked into my coat. I also spoke with them about the book I was writing for them and asked them to please guide me so that I could give them the voice they desired.

Additional offerings were made at Hel's altar in the lower *Ve* where I sang for my Dead, facing the Spirit Bridge as it arches off through the aethyr toward Scotland. The Sun had fallen below the western hills by the time we made our way toward the tree and great stone slab dedicated to Odin. When I came to the boundary, I paused to ask permission to enter, and then moved forward. While singing to Fire, I lit the candle I'd brought, then made *blót* to the All-Father, offering thanks for His instruction.

I wanted to dance, although my arthritic left knee and hip were hurting badly. So, I asked Eric to drum for me and showed him the tempo I wanted. At first I turned in circles, spiraling around the small trees that ring the cleared area, but my state was so altered that I struggled to stay on my feet. I finally staggered over to a wild cherry and anchored my energy through the tree. This allowed me to rise and shift my energy into my Owl body. I flapped for a while, flying over barren ground, then shifted into Reindeer, galloping across the tundra. Next, I shifted into Snake and crawled, then back into Owl again. It was all I could do to ground and get myself and my newly awakened coat back up the hill.

Each time I wear my coat in ceremony, the energy embodied in it gets stronger, and the simple act of putting it on now alters my state of consciousness. What began as a ritual garment has become an *ongon* or "spirit house," now with a personality of its own.

It has been my experience that when my work is aligned with what The Holy Powers desire of me, necessary tools and resources flow. On many occasions, I have been gifted out of the blue with an item soon necessary for a healing. I still experience these synchronicities as remarkable, and they fill me with wonder and gratitude.

Traditional shamanism relies on the practitioner's ability to access altered states of consciousness, and drums have always been an important tool for that work. For many years, I'd owned a seven-sided deerskin drum, but, for whatever reason, I found it difficult to accomplish what I needed to with it. I looked at many different styles of drums and eventually felt guided to visit the website of the couple who had made Raven's big drum. In a striking coincidence, their names were Erik and Suzanne, while my husband and I are Eric and Susannah. Their Sámi-style frame drums are created using wood harvested in the old way, assembled with reverence and care.

"Look for a drum with my skin and antlers," Reindeer instructed, but, each time that I found one that seemed right, it sold before I could purchase it. This led to a morning routine; I would sit down in front of my laptop with my coffee and open their website to see if "my" drum was there.

It became apparent that, after claiming me, Freyja had placed me in some sort of timeshare with Odin, deeming it safe for me to learn from The Old Man now that I had the benefit of Her protection. In a particularly powerful dream, He led me to the foot of great Yggdrasil and taught me many mysteries, ultimately handing me a curious key carved from Reindeer antler. I arose the next morning, went to Erik and Suzanne's website, and there at the top was a big ash-framed oval drum with a reindeer-hide head and reindeer antler handle shaped like a tree, named after the mighty World Tree ridden by the All-Father.

"I am your drum!" it announced emphatically as the image lit up.

How to scrape up the very substantial price?

Still, I emailed immediately to make the purchase. Time

and again, when I have acted in response to the call of the spirits, they have made available the resources to do their work. That afternoon, out of the blue, I received a major geomancy contract, the fee for which covered the cost of the drum perfectly.

I eagerly awaited my drum's arrival, hoping that it would arrive in conjunction with the autumn "Hunter's Moon." Past experience had shown me that items from overseas rarely arrive when anticipated, and the tracking information is somewhat vague. While working in the garden, I felt the urge to walk down the hill to the mailbox and was standing there when, a few minutes later, our postman arrived.

"Y'all got a package from Denmark," he announced.

In trance the evening before, I had been given a song with which to welcome and birth my drum. At moonrise, Eric and I kindled Sacred Fire, and I carefully opened the crate to reveal the rich purple velvet bag containing this wondrous and vibrantly alive tool. Blessed with the fragrant smoke of juniper, Yggdrasil was birthed in *galdr* and song and presented to the Holy Powers, a great drum for great work.

I have since journeyed to ask my drum how it wished to be decorated, and a rendering of the great World Tree now adorns its face, surrounded by the runes and images of many of my dearest allies. With this amazing drum, I call and move energy as well as access sacred realms, often riding the spirit of Reindeer with the North Wind at my back.

Nineteen
LINEAGE AND LEGACY

It is often the case in traditional shamanism that, as one moves more deeply into one's individual shamanic practice, one encounters taboos imposed by one's Holy Powers. Many of my colleagues have dietary restrictions, especially around artificial ingredients and inorganic foods. While some follow the shamanic path of Sacred Plants, others find that they are forbidden marijuana, alcohol, even coffee and non-herbal tea.

Initially, Freyja informed me that I would be limited to clothing of natural fibers: cotton, linen, rayon, Merino wool (I am allergic to other wools), and leather. Having long sewed much of my clothing, this wasn't problematic. There were instructions as to when I should or should not wear Freyja's amber, and, later, that, under many circumstances, I should cover my head, whether with a simple scarf or one of several ceremonial headpieces. The furs and bones of some animals are forbidden, while those of others are considered valued talismans. These taboos and commands are generally intended to support the practitioner and to bring them somehow into balance, both within themself and in alignment with their Holy Powers.

Knowing that I would not experience a formal initiation myself, I nevertheless wanted to see that future Guild members would have the benefit of meaningful ceremonies. During Raven's annual late winter visit, I spoke at length about the importance of ritual and the need to provide students with affirmation and encouragement. I wanted to help build a stronger Guild and a more effective training protocol.

More clients were finding me through my new website, asking for help ranging from house blessings to healing. In some cases, this requires the creation of deeply personal cere- monies, such as the one I devised to help two women release the legacy of alcoholism in their respective lineages. Addiction is a terrible thing, as I well knew from its impact in my own family.

I asked each of the women to find a grapefruit-sized stone willing to serve, write all they needed to about the impact of this legacy and the healing they hoped to find, and, then, bind paper to stone with yarn representing their *Wyrd*. At the scheduled time, my clients appeared, solemn and thoughtful.

We lit the torches and began in the upper *Ve* by hailing the Gods, Ancestors, *vaettir*, and allies with a horn full of apple cherry cider. We made an offering plate with lemons, oranges, summer berries, and flowers from the garden. From there, we descended the trail down to where a small cauldron rested on Hel's *hörgr*. I sang for Fire as Eric struck sparks to ignite the tinder.

Each woman in turn stood against our World Tree as I bound her to it with yarn unwound from her stone, passing it back to her after many turns. I marked the energy center in her throat with *Cweorth*, rune of the funeral pyre, and *galdred* the rune deep into her energy field. Then, using the shears, each cut herself free, gathered the severed strands of yarn and dropped them into the cauldron to be consumed by the flames.

When this was completed, we moved to the point of the knoll below the cliff, and I encouraged them to toss their stones out into the stream as I sang the Water Song. This was followed up with offerings of flowers and fruit to the water sprites and the *landvaettir* to thank them for their roles in the rite. Healing tears formed the final offering.

While my clients clung to each other, processing their experiences, I was carried into a vision wherein both Freyja and Odin spoke to me. In Her mellifluous voice, Freyja told me, "We pushed you forward over the past two years because you were needed. The working you just did not only aided in their healing but in your own. You've worked very hard this year dealing with the challenges We have laid before you. We want you to know that We recognize that this rite has marked your shift to the next level in your practice."

In a powerful lesson about my own issues with body dysmorphia, Odin followed up, gesturing at the body I had so despised, including the belly that had carried two amazing sons when I had never imagined I might have children. "We gave you the perfect body for this work, a vessel capable of carrying a great deal of power, comprised of both sexes and a gifted mind."

I cupped my belly in my hands, conscious of how I've always constricted it in an effort to make it smaller. All-Father scowled and, in an instant, I saw the bowl of my belly holding the vastness of the cosmos.

His deep voice boomed, "See! We made you so you could do that. Be the vessel We made you to be!"

Later that year, at the annual gathering, I shared with Raven Freyja's instruction that my elevation to Level Five be recognized. He appeared dubious, but the runes confirmed this guidance.

The following spring, I accepted my first two apprentices, both brilliant, focused, and having a strong connection to the Gods and their Ancestors. Divination offers significant insight into whether an applicant has the qualities I look for, and Freyja was clear with me that I was to follow my instincts. As I reflected on my frustration with the lack of support and constructive critical feedback during my own training, I determined to be much more engaged as an instructor. I made myself readily available to my apprentices, one in Texas and the other in Arizona. We shared in-depth correspondence, phone conferences, and each came for intensive training at TwoTrees the following spring. I quickly realized how much I love teaching.

Ken Bradstock and I often met for tea. He, with his years of experience, offered much welcome guidance and encouragement, helping me clarify not only my own practice but also the values I wanted to impart to my students. Remembering my own longing for formal recognition of my apprenticeship and ceremonies marking the achievement of each training level, I initiated the practice of celebrating the relationship between Teacher and Apprentice through ceremony as a significant rite of passage.

Eric and I decided to prepare for spring with a *Disting* celebration that included the old Anglo Saxon tradition of "Charming the Plough." *Disting* is a rite honoring our Foremothers and maternal bloodline, also referred to as the *Desir*. The ritual of Charming the Plough prepares farming equipment for opening the Earth Mother. Eric and I talked about what we wanted to do and finally gathered up our gardening tools (spades, hoes, rakes, and tiller) and hauled them to the upper *Ve*, our space sacred to the Vanic Gods of Harvest. Eric filled a big bucket of warm water while I rounded up a scrub brush, a bottle of beer, and a bottle of our lemon-ginger cordial. We also took green and yellow ribbons to adorn the tools and honor Freyr and Freyja, Lord and Lady of Vanaheim. After the previous week's intense winter storm, the day held a definite hint of spring to come, being sunny and well into the 60's. The Little Sisters were active at their hives, and I offered a quick blessing over them.

Once in the upper *Ve*, we welcomed the Gods and honored

the *landvaettir* and our *Desir*. Then we washed the tools in the water, making them clean and ready for use while indicating our respect for the Earth and a commitment to be good stewards. When all were cleansed, we dressed each of them, tying on fluttering lengths of green and yellow ribbon in honor of Freyr and Freyja. Next, we spoke a blessing over each tool as I called upon the spirit of *Jera*, the rune of Nature's cycles and the fruitful harvest, while Eric poured a drought of beer over the blade of the implement. When this was done, we poured a measure of the cordial, honey-sweet essence of summer, into the horn and hailed the Gods, the land, and our foremothers; we drank and offered the remainder over the stone *hörgr* that serves as an altar.

In early April, I dreamed of saplings piled together in a cone, teepee fashion, their tops bound with rope and fluttering with blue silk prayer scarves.

A voice said, "Build an *adak*!"

When I got up the next morning, I recalled that *adak* is a Mongolian word for a votive structure to which silk or cotton scarves called *khadag* are imbued with prayers and intention and tied. Although sometimes special sacred trees become *adaks*, more often an *adak* is constructed as I dreamed, that is, with three supporting poles forming a tripod against which others are laid. In Mongolia, birch saplings are most often used, but I immediately thought of our red cedar, with its naturally preserving sap.

But I'm not Mongolian, I thought, puzzled.

My spirits replied, "But some of your ancient ancestors were. All over the world, people have built structures to honor the Holy Powers as they understand them. Why not you, *bagshagui*? We did not call and teach you to be a cultural purist; rather, to be competent and to serve."

As I sat with my dream, I was told to ask trees to present

themselves and that I could only take living trees willing to participate. It was also clear that the *adak* should be raised near the community sacred space we were developing, located in the now wooded bottomland that was the analog to the rune pool of my dreams and dedicated to Odin.

On the designated day, the spring Sun broke from behind Hemlock Ridge, turning the tender, emerging foliage brilliant gold-green. Eric and I loaded the tools we would need into my car and drove down the hill. Because the project merged elements of both Mongolian practice and the Northern Traditions, it seemed right that we should plan for a total of nine saplings, a number of significance for both. We followed the winding trail under river birches, sourwoods, and aging pines, stepping over the lush dark mounds of Christmas fern, ferrying saws and axes and offerings. Once we'd gotten to the clearing, I began to wander the area, singing a little chant to call for participants. I softened my focus and just wandered until a cedar called out to me. Then, I went to it, offered tobacco, laid my hands on the trunk, and prayed:

> *Brother Cedar, I give thanks for your beauty*
> *And for the food and shelter you have provided.*
> *Send forth your life force into other trees nearby,*
> *That they be strengthened.*
> *I honor the gift of your body for our holy Adak.*

When I felt that the spirit of the tree had abandoned it, Eric cut it down, and I trimmed away the boughs until we had the bare trunk. We marked and sawed 10-foot lengths and dragged them back to Odin's *Ve* to dry.

On a warm May afternoon, accompanied by one of my apprentices who had come up from Texas for several intense days, we gathered to raise the *adak*, our hands filled with sky blue silk prayer flags. We lit a small sacred fire with flint and steel and offered prayers for our intentions for the rite. Then, we took our respective *khatag* and went off to pray over them.

When the time felt right, I put on my shaman's coat and sang to call power. In the traditional way, I sprinkled the three primary poles with milk to bless them. Tying them together, we each took one and raised the foundation tripod. I continued praying, blessing the other poles and the circle formed by the tripod in the same fashion. We took turns tying on our *khatag* until all nine poles were situated in a ceremony that proved surprisingly deep and sweet.

Later that month, Eric and I made a trip to the state park where I spent my childhood. It was the first time I'd been back since my dad's memorial in 2010. The overt reason was for me to donate his dress uniform to the park service, which still uses the old-style uniforms for formal occasions. As we drove into the park, the memories rolled over me. We crept by the little house I had grown up in and around through the woods where I'd spent every possible free moment. As I prayed softly for a sign my shamanic work was on track, a female Barred Owl, one of my primary allies, swooped in front of us, gliding silently from tree to tree, leading us to the field where I'd so often played as a child. The remarkable encounter answered my prayer.

We spent a couple of hours visiting with the current superintendent and a pair of his rangers, swapping tales and answering some of their questions about what it was like "back then" before enjoying a picnic lunch in the spot where my family often had dined together so long ago. The park had changed a lot through the years. Yet, in many ways, it remained the place that shaped me so profoundly.

Before leaving, I wanted to make an offering to the *landvaettir*, so we stopped at the park gate where there are huge boulders I played on while awaiting the school bus. With Eric in tow, I walked back into the forest a short way to where a cleft in one of the boulders formed a natural basin. There, I poured out water and offered tobacco. While praying, I had the distinct sense of eyes on me, and, looking up, I spotted a huge Broadhead skink in the full russet glory of his mating colors, gazing at me. Eric and I stood very still as the big lizard wandered around on the stones, and I began to do something I did as a child: I "called" him to me. We often encounter Broadheads at TwoTrees, and their instinct is invariably to run away. But this guy circled closer and closer as I held my energy still and spoke softly and calmingly. Eventually, he closed the four-foot gap to come right to my feet, staring up at me with small bright eyes.

"Thank you!" I said, through tears of wonder, and it was as if I'd released him from a spell: he turned and dashed away.

It felt good to know that I've still got the mojo, even if I don't know exactly what I'm actually doing. Lizards have the ability to drop and then regenerate the ends of their tails when captured by a predator. That led me to thinking about my own efforts at self-healing in the aftermath of assaults and traumas. Many spirit traditions also consider Lizard the indicator to pay attention to one's dreams and trust one's intuition—again, something that rings true for me.

I continued to learn from my tools and spirits, filling in the many gaps in my human training. Although aware that the Sámi had used their sacred drums as tools for divination, I had never attempted anything like this myself. If Necessity is the Mother of Invention, She is also the shaman's teacher. I was engaged to cleanse and bless a large home with numerous rooms, closets, and cul-de-sacs. There were many places where miasma had accumulated until it was quite tangible. The spaces where electronics were densest (for example, where the home wifi internet router was located or the closet with the whole-house sound system controls) had the greatest concentration of negative, unwholesome energy. Because the homeowners were concerned that I might scatter sparks or damage woodwork with water, I couldn't use smoke or asperge, but I could use my drum Yggdrasil to break up and clear bad energy, while introducing and reinforcing positive energy.

I quickly discovered that I could also use the drum as a way of sensing or diagnosing when the energy was gunky. I could drum, and, in clear areas, the tone would ring on in a very bell-like way. In places where the energy was stale or heavy or foul, the drum's tone became dull and muted. So, I moved around each space, striking the drum, facing it high and low, and listening to changes in the tone. Then, I *galdred* cleansing runes and drummed as seemed appropriate until I could get the clear tone. It had never occurred to me that a drum might be used diagnostically in that way, but it became a welcome addition to my toolkit and certainly proved helpful.

My client sits across the table from me at a folding wooden table once belonging to my mother's mother. Prior to his arrival, I cleansed the room: swept and dusted and recaned with the spicy smoke of sacred rosemary, lit candles, and made offerings at my altars. The table is draped with a hand-dyed lapis blue covering I have sewn, embedding prayers with each stitch. I offer a prayer to hallow the act of divination and invite my client to do the same. And then, they ask their question, this thing they struggle with, and ask me to seek guidance for.

I straighten my back, aligning my body with the tug of gravity, breathing deeply to draw in energy for the work. A soft brown deer-skin bag holds my runes, thirty-three enspirited symbols that I have carved into rectangles of bone and stained with red ocher and my own blood. Unbinding the bag, I breathe in the scent of the leather and offer my life-breath as my gift to these allies. Now, to form the link: Cradling the heavy pouch in my left hand, I reach in and sift the cool bone tablets between the fingers of my right as I rock and hum, rock and hum, falling into the soft space of Knowing.

One by one, runes come into my hand to be placed in a particular position on the table before me. Or, sometimes, I'm guided to simply take up a handful and throw them down to fall willy-nilly, awaiting my interpretation of their messages. In a low voice, I share the information revealed before me – the information that this mildly altered state of consciousness allows me to access – and offer guidance.

The previous passage describes what I think of as widening my bandwidth a bit, the shift in consciousness I experience when communicating with my Holy Powers: the Gods, Ancestors, and spirits I serve and work with. It varies in the level of dissociation that comes with it, and, when I am in it, I may or may not be especially aware of what's going on around me or what I'm doing or saying.

At its most extreme, as in when I serve as a *Spaekona* or trance medium, song and movement carry me into an altered state that progresses to a sense that I am filled with rushing light. I experience the feeling that I am falling over backwards (although I don't), and, then, I am gone, totally unaware of the guidance or wisdom that flows through me until I am ritually called back into myself.

This returning comes with an understandable sense of great vulnerability. When I come out of a deep trance, it's almost like struggling to awaken from deep sleep. Great effort is involved, and then I am famished and exhausted and hyper-sensitive to noise. Eric has learned to have cheese and chicken, fruit and nuts available for me immediately afterwards. Such deep trance states are draining, and I have learned that I must pace myself.

Where would my gifts and skills lead me?

Summer crept in, a heavy, moist blanket across the Carolina Piedmont, and I continued in intense self-assessment. On the summer solstice I wrote:

Longest day,
Shine deep into me,
Your honey-warmth
Illuminating my darkest corners —
Those places where fears still bind me,
Where ignorance limits me,
Where resentment weighs me down.
Airless, dusty places in my soul
That might be better used:
A garden, perhaps,
Or a nook to read again a much loved tale,
An afternoon to fill with a grandchild's laughter.
Daystar, reign late into the evening,
That I may dance amidst the fireflies,
And triumph over my own darkness.

Twenty
TIME TO CLEAN HOUSE

Many Core shamans work in their street clothes, and I have been told I look absurd in my deerskin coat and antler head-piece, but I deeply value the assistance and protection of my regalia in the more difficult aspects of my work. Shamanism is a service profession, and I am often called upon to deal with the impact of spirits, ghosts, and fouled energy on land, homes, and their residents. Many things exist outside the bounds of what our society considers "real," as well understood by animist Indigenous cultures. Some of those things are troublesome or even dangerous, as I learned in one particularly challenging undertaking.

I was approached by a young couple in the first year of their marriage who related that they experienced significant discomfort in certain areas of their rented home. Yet, they could find no concrete reason for their anxiety. Over time, despite therapy, the tension between them had increased until they began to consider separating. The husband was suspicious that something about the house was exacerbating their conflicts and asked me to assess the energy in the space and clear it, if possible. I agreed and began to prepare for this task.

As is often the case with shamanic workings, once I commit, I begin to receive information intuitively regarding the client, circumstances of the site where I will be working, or other relevant insights, often coming in the form of visions of events that were significant in shaping the client or the energetic fabric of the site. This up-front knowledge helps me plan what tools and supplies I will need, including candles, offerings, salt, or other cleansing materials. I also typically bring sacred herbs for recaning, my tradition's version of what is commonly called smudging, and my coat and drum, which calls ally spirits to my assistance and allows me to shatter and clear away negative energy.

The house had been cleared of almost all personal belongings, and, upon arrival, I advised the couple I wanted to form my own impressions. The small house was divided into a kitchen, living/dining area, two bedrooms, a bath, and a laundry room. The stairway to the basement opened to the attic above, and the basement itself was a warren of strange rooms. Behind the house was a separate garage. After the walk-through, I shared my perceptions with the tenants and, then, asked for theirs. We found we were in total agreement about numerous places that felt off and sometimes even threatening.

As I always do before engaging in a working, I kindled Sacred Fire and did some divination, using my runes to know whether to proceed, and, if so, how to do so. This also confirmed my intuitive read: We were dealing with a house constructed shortly after the Second World War over a natural feature that amplified negative energies—a house that was the site of a suicide and that, by its very design, collected and augmented negative energy.

I taught the young couple a simple exercise to shield themselves so that nothing I mobilized during the working could attach to any of us. Then, I asked the husband to light charcoal tablets in my heavy clay censer for a mixture of finely ground mugwort, myrrh, dragon's blood resin, and copal resin that I had previously prepared, and, then, to fan the resulting smoke into all spots where the energy felt dense or unclean.

As is my practice, I began with songs to hail the Holy Powers, honor my Ancestors, call power, and, finally, to wake up my drum. I moved counterclockwise, the direction of banishing, around the room, drumming and galdring the rune Cweorth *(sign of the*

funeral pyre). The effect of this was to break up old congealed ener-
gy (mostly of a fearful, depressive nature) and push it ahead of me.
Periodically, as the energetic debris piled up, I also ululated to clear
it. I drum instinctively, choosing rhythms, where on the drum head I
strike and whether to also incorporate strikes of the beater against the
drum frame. Typically, the greater the energetic resistance I encoun-
ter, the more forceful and complex my drumming pattern becomes.

I was careful to work the corners, behind doors and in closets,
working through the upstairs in the same pattern. When I came to
the kitchen, the energy was particularly bad, and the wife noted that
she avoided entering whenever possible. I had them open all the cab-
inets and recan each of them as well as the space above them where
there was the sense of something crouching.

From there, we progressed to the small laundry room, where I
turned on the sink tap and galdred Laguz, *the rune of Flow, to help*
flush away what we had pushed out of the kitchen. Upon opening the
door to the stairs, I could feel that a "feeder" spirit was crouched over
the opening into the attic, just where it could dine on the anxiety of
anyone descending into the creepy basement. I galdred the rune Isa
(Ice) to block and freeze it in place, and we carefully went downstairs
to the basement, which was divided up into a series of dark, low-ceil-
inged, spaces that felt angry, despairing, and self-destructive. I had
the distinct sense that the house vaettir *or main house spirit, which*
was anchored in a central brick pillar, desperately wanted to be any-
where else, reinforcing my initial intuition that the house had been
built over some natural sump of negative energy.

As the basement of a house is an analog for the human uncon-
scious, I had to work much harder here to shift the accumulation of
negativity. At one point, while I was focused on drumming and my
inner perceptions, the angry spirit struck back with a shove. My
right foot snagged against the stub of a pipe set into the concrete
floor, nearly tripping me and, as I later discovered, breaking a toe.
A vortex of foul, dark energy stretched from the open pipe upward

through the house and into the attic. We continued on to a small room that the husband had used as a workspace. It was directly under the kitchen. This and the furnace room were the primary problematic loci in the house.

I found myself having to resort to much more complex rhythms that included sharp percussive knocks on the drum rim with the beater. A strange harmonic vibration built up that sounded almost like a low wailing. This was a phenomenon I had never before encountered, and one that was later remarked upon by my clients. I moved back into the main furnace room, where I opened a Portal and forced the gunk through before closing it.

By this point I was very clear that the primary problem, in addition to the site, was the energetic residue left by a suicide on the property. I had felt within the house the slow disintegration of a man: the particular tang of alcoholism and financial failure, compounded by the abandonment of a divorce. We walked across the sunny backyard to the garage, and I paused before entering, scanning the plants near me and asking for an ally. A stalk of rabbit tobacco, a liminal plant long associated by Native American people with calling back living spirits and banishing dead ones, stood glowing nearby. Upon my request, it gave me permission to take it. I paused at the entrance and laid the plant stem across the doorway with my thanks.

Upon stepping into the garage, I could clearly see the space in use as a machine shop by the problematic owner. The time was the early 1970s, shortly after the Vietnam War, and the ghost in question had been a veteran who suffered extensively from PTSD. In an effort to self-medicate, he resorted to alcohol with the result that his marriage and life spiraled out of control, culminating in divorce and bankruptcy. I experienced a clear vision of the man, dressed in an oil-stained green coverall, placing a revolver to his temple, and pulling the trigger. His blood soaked into the concrete floor, anchoring his troubled spirit in place. I did what I could to help him pass over and find peace but cautioned the young couple that it was impossible to completely clear the energy of the tragedy from the space and recommended that they keep their encounters there to an absolute minimum.

As we reentered the house through the outside door to the laundry room, I found myself face-to-face with the "feeder" spirit, which I had frozen in the attic portal above the stairs. At this time, I galdred runes to wall off the spirit in the attic, creating a strong boundary and slowly dissipating this predator.

Once we were back in the house and I had removed my regalia, I did follow-up divination to make sure my work had addressed the issues of the site. I recommended that small dishes of salt be placed in each of the cabinets, closets, and under the bed. I directed that the black salt I provided be sprinkled along each window sill and the threshold of each outer door. My clients related that afterwards the house felt noticeably different, lighter, and more peaceful. Even their dog was calmer. This sort of intensive work could not have been accomplished without my coat and drum.

Although I had several jewelry commissions in the queue, I often seemed to be stuck, sitting at my bench in a fog. The energetic architecture of my studio had been the same for a number of years, and it no longer felt attuned to me or my current work. Determined to clear and reset the space, I donned my shaman's coat and hat. Carrying my drum, I walked along the path to the studio accompanied by the chiming of dozens of bells. Then, I removed my sandals at the door. After grounding and a brief prayer to the *landvaettir* and the Duergar, I lit rosemary incense and *galdred* the directions, tracing each rune with the glowing stick. Seeing the lines of force light up, I began to drum and sing at a rather brisk pace, building energy until it felt complete. I knew from experience that the energy would grow more complex over time, but at least it felt clean and clear.

I didn't think I'd run through all that much juice, but, by afternoon, I was shaky and unfocused. As is so often the case when energy is repurposed, something shifted. The following morning, I received a message from a friend wanting to know whether I would be willing to let her purchase an expensive major sculptural piece by installments – due to the price, I had never expected to find a buyer. Convinced that this was a result of energy freed up due to the studio cleansing, I gave thanks to Andvari and the Duergar.

Many hours were devoted to working on the manuscript for *The Duergarbok* in preparation for publication. Prompted by the Duergar to explore a new craft, I began carving small votive images of the Northern Gods. My father had been a skilled carver, and I often found myself recalling techniques he had imparted years before.

One urgent night,
I was overtaken by a sharp and unfamiliar spirit,
And wide and restless magic came upon me.

Across the years I watched my father
Stand before rough blocks of oak and linden,
Seeking the hidden creatures within,
His great gnarled hands
Tenderly freeing each neck and leg.

Like many another child before me,
I must carry on my father's work,
And so, I am drawn, not to familiar tools,
To paint or cloth or metal,

But to a staff of willow and a short, sharp knife.

Commanded to take up this craft,
I tense my hands,
Broad and competent like his,
And search mute wood for hidden treasure.

In this moment,
I am my father's vessel
And his spirit sings to me from the wood.

Twenty-One
INTO THE WILDERNESS

In the summer of 2019, the Northern Shamanism Guild gathered for Keepers Crossing at a large log house in rural Ohio, a central location for the participants. For the first time, I was to participate as an Elder with my own apprentices present. The large community altar we created to honor numerous Northern Gods occupied a big chunk of the living room, and one of my apprentices was elevated a level during the opening ceremony. Numerous workshops and classes were presented by the participants. Evenings were marked by ceremonies followed by noisy discussions. Still, something felt awry, and numerous occurrences served to underline how fundamentally different my approach had become from the rest of the Guild.

Afterwards, my apprentices expressed their discomfort with the event and the lack of respect accorded me as an Elder. My spirit guidance and practice had clearly carried me in a different direction. After much prayer and divination, I reached the difficult realization that the time had come for me to walk my own road. There was just one problem: I had agreed to host the initiation of one of Raven's apprentices at TwoTrees.

The negotiations surrounding the ceremony were fraught, as I felt pressure from Raven over the timing, and had to consider numerous commitments of my own. I decided to journey in hope of gaining guidance from Freyja. The imagery began with my standard induction: I envisioned myself paddling a canoe up a narrow slough overhung by birches and willows. I rowed for some time, eventually entering a lake. In time, I was swept up into the flow of a very fast river and abruptly found myself going over a waterfall. I sank deep and began to swim down, entering a hole that opened into a cave. As I bobbed in the cold water, I could see Freyja facing a fire with Her back to me, the light from the flames leaping and dancing on the cave wall. When She turned to face me, I saw Her in Her fierce and war-like visage. I humbly asked for guidance.

"Be true to yourself," She said forcefully.

I held my boundaries, negotiated, and, early in November, Raven and I initiated H. with the support of those near and dear to her, beloved friends who had driven down from Michigan to feast and celebrate. I had fulfilled my commitment to the Guild and there would now be someone within the group to carry the thread of my lineage. The following day, as the three of us met at my old oak table, I announced that my relationship with the Northern Shamanism Guild would be changing: I would take on a different role as ally and independent affiliate. I had learned a lot from Raven — most importantly that I needed to teach and work in my own way, empowering and supporting my students and serving my local community.

People clearly hunger for the Sacred, for rites of passage and ceremonies that connect them to the Earth, to the Seasons, and to their Ancestors – a connection missing in our modern world. 18 Springs in nearby Winston Salem offered an excellent opportunity to engage with the wider community. I was invited to participate in a series of presentations by individuals from different spiritual paths, which offered me the opportunity to clarify how my specialist shamanism differed from the shamanic practices of others. I also taught a well-received class on the sacred art of divination and how practitioners could improve their signal clarity.

Given that my practice blends elements of several shamanic traditions, I am occasionally confronted by self-righteous purists calling the legitimacy of my work into question. Ours is a culture that places more emphasis on credentials than on competency and confuses the acquisition of the one for the other.

I remind them that cultures have always encountered and blended with other cultures. "I serve the Gods and spirits that speak to me and that are willing to work with me," I tell them.

What matters is the work.

With the news filled with dire reports of thawing permafrost, Reindeer and other northern spirits pleaded for me to do something to help raise awareness of global warming. In response, I organized a Rite for the Arctic. The ceremony, anchored by a huge, slowly melting block of candle-lit ice, recognized the importance of 52 different inhabitants and components of the Arctic biosphere and offered participants the opportunity to learn and grieve.

A few weeks later, I was invited to raise an *adak* at 18 Springs. A dozen stout bamboo poles were provided, and I brought milk for offering and a bundle of deep blue *khatags*. The afternoon was very cold but sunny, and we were eventually joined by about a dozen well-bundled women and several children. I donned my coat and beaded head-covering and began to explain about myself and my tradition, what an *adak* was, and what we would each be doing.

I began by tying a rainbow scarf to the longest pole, identifying myself as intersex and offering my prayer that our world might become a place where people can live as whatever gender they identify with. Then, Eric and I tied the Grandmother, Grandfather, and Grandchild poles that represent community. As we held each pole, the participants breathed their prayers into their scarves, speaking them aloud, occasionally weeping as they tied their *khata* on the poles.

Prayers for healing, for the poor, for racial justice, for hope.

One woman brought prayer ties made from her daughter's old pillowcases, bright with multicolored peace symbols. The process was orderly but went on for a long time as there were many prayers to be shared. As each pole grew heavy with *khatags*, we stood it against the central three, making a brightly colored teepee-shaped prayer tree. I offered milk and song, and everyone joined in. After all, a shaman serves a community; my heart was full.

Perhaps most importantly, I was finding balance. My work is rooted in Ancestral shamanic practices, yet it is flexible and adaptive to our modern world.

"Will you be leading a Yule Ceremony at 18 Springs?" The inquiries poured in through email and social media.

As always, it was a challenge to find a balance between my own Heathen faith and creating a ritual that would be meaningful and accessible for the majority. Hot wassail, cookies, candlelight, and the Sámi-inspired music of the Norwegian choral ensemble Cantus helped set the mood as I spoke of the solstice as a time to reset and release – and of why we should value darkness. The lights were dimmed and I described how our ancient ancestors would have celebrated this longest night. Then, I led everyone into a period of stillness, as we sat together in the dark surrounded by beautiful music and goodwill.

The turn-out for the ceremony was great, with many of those attending being folks I had never seen or met before. The donations collected went toward the scholarship fund. The following morning, as we have for most solstices over the past 24 years, Eric and I drove up to Pilot Mountain to "Sing up the Sun." This year, we were not to celebrate alone.

It was a balmy 34 degrees this Yule, and we were struck by how much the ecosystem of the mountain has been changed by the forest fire that occurred three years ago, leaving the pinnacles almost bare. In the first years of our celebrations, we often found the weather on the mountain bitter and icy, and there was never anyone else about. The gate would open at 7 a.m., allowing us to climb to the Little Pinnacle just as Sunna emerged from the intersection of the Big Pinnacle and the horizon. Moving in her arc across the morning sky, the Sun was briefly held between the twin trunks of a wind-sculpted pine, now gone. Such an ephemeral yet wondrous phenomenon!

Today, the mountain was abustle with a race, and runners being shuttled from the base of the mountain to the trailhead. Still, there was no one present on the Little Pinnacle when we arrived. Our ceremonies over the years have grown simpler, although no less heartfelt. I hailed the Holy Powers in song and poured out milk, then offered tobacco. As I did so, I could hear footsteps coming up behind us and determined to complete my ceremony.

Afterward, we turned to greet the newcomer, a young man who apologized for interrupting us. We assured him he was welcome and explained our history of honoring the solstice in this way. In turn, he explained that he'd recently left the military and had come down from Washington, DC, to visit his mother in the eastern part of the state before heading out to explore the country. It turned out that he'd missed out on celebrating the solstice with his friends in DC, so it seemed altogether appropriate for him to do so with us. He mentioned that he was keeping a journal of his adventures and asked to take our picture so that he could share about meeting us. Just a lovely encounter...

To my delight, *The Duergarbok: The Dwarves in the Northern Tradition* was finally published by Asphodel Press, the handsome cover adorned with the Norse belt buckle I had created for Eric's Yule gift three years previously. Plans were underway for a book-signing celebration at 18 Springs. I felt deep satisfaction to have fulfilled my commitment to share the stories of the Duergar, Master Makers of the North. Somehow, the birthing of this book seemed a fitting culmination to my half-century as a sacred smith. After much struggle, I concluded that it was time for me to close Jewels of the Spirit and retire as a jeweler, although this was a heart-wrenching decision for me. Aging had brought blurred vision that glasses could not correct, and a benign tremor in my hands made it impossible for me to manage the fine details that had always been the hallmarks of my work.

At Yule, Kristy had given me a lovely deerskin pouch with the image of one of the horse paintings from the cave at Lascaux, thinking rightly that it would compliment my horse-spirited shaman's coat. The spirit of Horse is one of movement and power, representing the personal sovereignty I had worked so hard to claim. Although I had never made a drum, I found myself called to undertake this project with a surprising urgency.

This will be your journey drum, Horse told me.

I acquired a ten-inch frame made from Western Red Cedar, the same wood Eric used in my *vaettir kista*, and I purchased a piece of uncured horse rawhide.

When the new Moon arrived, I began by recaning both the frame and the hide with the fragrant smoke of rosemary to cleanse and enliven them, while greeting them with songs of welcome and gratitude. The stiff, dry rawhide drumhead and lacings soaked overnight in a basin of water to rehydrate until slippery and supple, and I sanded the drum frame to silky smoothness before rubbing red ochre I'd ground to a fine powder into the wood to stain it a deep red-brown, followed by layer after layer of wax from our bees, buffed to a soft sheen.

The next morning, I marked and punched the lacing holes in the drum head and set about stretching it over the frame, lacing back and forth across the back of the drum, gradually pulling the head taut. The process is challenging and yet rewarding, drawing one into collaboration with the Beings of Horse and Tree. When I was finally satisfied that I'd pulled the damp lacings as tightly and evenly as possible, I placed the little drum next to one of the heat vents and waited for the magic to happen, for it is only as a drum dries that it awakens, and you learn its voice.

While waiting, I peeled and sanded a short length of hazel, a wood considered protective and sacred in my tradition. I wound woolen yarn around and around one end. Using a needle and sewing thread, I then stitched back and forth through the wool until I had tacked and secured it into a ball-like beater end. The result was firm and springy. The following morning I awoke to find a lightweight little drum with a bright, almost bell-like tone. Using mineral pigments, I painted her with a galloping and very pregnant horse, framed by a spiral and the glyph for water.

The next day, after my usual cycle of prayers and offerings, I took up the drum and set a fast, racing beat. Almost immediately I had a vivid image of the wide steppe grasslands of Mongolia, rolling hills to the far horizon with a vast blue sky scattered with fluffy clouds. My *hame* or energy body began to shift into the form of a dun-colored stallion with black mane, tail, and legs. I began to gallop, calling to my mares to run with me. I continued this experience for some minutes, just enjoying being in a horse body and the power of movement.

When I was done, I recalled my childhood fascination with horses and the sense of wonder I'd always felt being carried by one of these magnificent Beings. Over the next weeks, it became clear that each of my three drums had particular uses. My original seven-sided drum, now bearing the name Tekka (Finnish for "Woodpecker"), became a drum students could handle. The big reindeer drum Yggdrasil is best at healing and manipulating energy and allows no-one but me to touch him. The little horse drum has proved perfect for journeying.

In addition to enspirited physical tools and alliances, I knew I needed the most important tool of all: discernment. Requests for shamanic services continued to come in, ranging from divination work to inquiries from those who believed that they were themselves called by the spirits to become shamans. Working with Ken and my therapist, I continued to clarify the boundaries between shamanic gifts and delusion— both for myself and for those persons who sought my skills.

The ready access to information via the Internet is both blessing and bane, as many who are bewildered encounter information that frames all sorts of challenging experiences as being the result of "Spiritual Emergence." It has been my experience that many of these individuals, while possibly possessing some psychic aptitude, also struggle with vari-ous forms of mental illness and desperately desire any other explanation for the strange phenomena they experience. Still, I always treat them with respect and do the necessary divina-tion to assess whether or not they are truly called. I provide appropriate support when I can and recommend resources and reading materials. Sadly, I often have to tell them that their needs are above my pay grade.

Being called to such an uncommon profession brings with it many challenges. In another time and among other people, I would know fellow practitioners sharing my beliefs, skills, and frame of reference — colleagues I could consult or refer to. Clients seeking me out would have some idea of what to expect.

A woman has reached out to me. She believes that one of her ancestors was cursed, and, perhaps, that's why her life has been so hard. In her initial email, she tells me she experiences many strange illnesses, and she thinks spirits speak to her. We arrange to meet in a neutral office space. While I see some clients in my home at TwoTrees, I am very selective about allowing those visits.

She sits before me, her body curled inward. She's clearly uncertain, and her depression is tangible, a heavy field of miasma that rides her like a fog bank.

I smile and ask her how I can be of help.

"I want to understand what's happening to me. These voices, the things I see and know. I've done some research on the Internet, and I think I'm suffering from shaman sickness." Her distress is apparent, her eyes darting about but rarely engaging mine. "I hear these voices that I think are spirits. Sometimes, they want me to give messages to other people."

"Why don't you tell me a little about your life?"

I ask gentle questions about her history, and, as she opens up, I study the subtle energy field that surrounds her, especially around her head. I hold my bag of runes in my lap, discreetly pulling the bone tiles for guidance. The spirits in the runes, important allies whom I've wooed and fed regularly, indicate that the "curse" in her family is a pattern of dysfunction and abuse that extends back many generations — not some foul enchantment laid on them by an enemy.

"Sometimes I just know things," she explains. "The voices tell me stuff; they give me the messages. Isn't that how it is with sha-mans?"

I summon my tact. "Well, yes and no. It's been my experience that people can have real intuitive gifts but also have psychological difficulties. Do you work with a therapist?"

She shakes her head. "I did for a while, but I moved."

"Have you ever been on any kind of medication for mental health issues?"

Her eyes snap up and dart away from mine. I know that look, the look that tells me that she fears being judged and discounted. "Well, I was for awhile, but I stopped taking it."

I nod. I hear this far too often.

"Trouble affording it?"

She fidgets.

"Yeah. But mostly, I felt all shut down and isolated. When I took it, the spirits got mad and wouldn't talk to me."

The runes I pull tell me that while she has some intuitive ability, she definitely isn't called as a shaman. I share that information. She looks like she's about to cry.

I study her subtle energy field. To my inner sight, it looks muddy with multicolor streamers snaking around from the back of her head. This is something I've come to associate with persons struggling with schizophrenia. I am no psychotherapist, so I cannot ethically or legally diagnose her, but hers is a story I encounter often.

It is true that shamanic gifts occur on a continuum with many mental health disorders. This is complex and requires the perspective of trained professionals to parse out. Most people would rather have any justification for the strange things they experience than to be told they are mentally ill.

I talk with her a bit, then I recommend a book that explains how to ground and center and shield. These are all innocuous skills she may find helpful. I also tell her about some community resources and *encourage her to find a shamanism-friendly therapist who can better assist her in teasing apart her voices. As the hour comes to an end, I thank her for having the courage to reach out.*

"I just want to help people," *she declares mournfully.*

"I know. And maybe the place to start is to get yourself sorted first."

The new year was born, and I did as I have long done, engaging in divination in an effort to get a heads-up on what might lie ahead. This year, the runes cautioned of obstacles and blockages, challenges in communication and in health, of losses and isolation. *Hagalaz*, the hail rune, was prominent. All the signs said that 2020 was going to be a doozie.

The previous summer, aware of his failing health, Ken had asked if I would be willing to minister to his family when he died, a task I felt inadequate to take on. He'd been hospitalized a couple of times in the fall for what had been diagnosed as congestive heart failure, and we both knew his time was limited. I repeatedly tried to get him to define what he meant by "minister," but never made much progress.

"You'll know," he affirmed. "Just get the story. People heal when they tell their stories."

I knew the truth of this wisdom; sharing my own story with him had done much to heal me.

I hadn't seen Ken since early November, when he'd spent a marvelous afternoon at TwoTrees, laughing and wise-cracking. He put down his mug of peppermint tea, rich with our honey, and his warm voice grew more solemn. "Susannah, have you given some thought to what I asked of you?"

I could see his great life-force was ebbing.

"I have, and I am willing," I replied.

"Good. I'm glad. And, thank you." He nodded and rose to leave.

At the door, he drew me into one of his wonderful bear hugs.

"I love you," I told him unselfconsciously.

Life is short and uncertain.

"I know. And, I love you, too," he responded.

Shortly after Thanksgiving, I had developed a respiratory bug, and, as much as I wanted to see Ken, I was afraid of passing it to him. We texted a little and messaged through Facebook; I mailed him a copy of *The Duergarbok*, knowing that he, also a writer, was happy for me.

In late January, I dreamed of standing in my grandmother's empty house while a hearse parked outside. When my phone rang the following morning, I saw Ken's name and knew he was gone. In a tremulous voice, his wife confirmed my hunch and asked whether I would be willing to perform his memorial service. Apparently, he had gone out to his little office, where their son later found him peacefully slumped in his chair.

On a day dark with rain and sleet, I listened to many wonderful stories about my friend and, then, led a celebration of his remarkable life. Immediately prior to the service, which turned out to be much more of a funeral than a brief memorial, I learned I was expected to lead the family in a prayer, something I had no preparation for whatsoever. Ken definitely didn't consider himself a Christian, but I knew that other family members were. So, I did my best to create a prayer around the power of love that connects us all – a love that was so strong in Ken.

He was such an extraordinary man, making every person he met feel like they were the most special friend he had. He had an amazing gift for listening and encouraging you to share yourself, which made you feel truly Seen and Heard. He had a great, booming laugh, a wonderful sense of humor, and a brilliant, inquisitive mind. I've never known anyone who so embodied Love. So that was the thread around which I built the service. The hardest part was managing my own grief and loss so that I could be open for others and officiate without breaking down.

As I sat at the pulpit looking down on his flag-draped casket (he'd been a Marine), I thought, *Damn it, Bear — you really threw me in the deep end of the pond with this one!*

And, I imagined I heard that laugh and saw his eyes twinkling.

...And you swam beautifully!

Twenty-Two
SPIRITUAL ARCHAEOLOGY

In late January of 2020, I wrote in my journal,

> The World Health Organization has reported an outbreak of a severe respiratory virus related to SARS in China. Although the Chinese government claims to be addressing the epidemic and our own government is dismissive of the threat, I am overwhelmed by the strong premonition that this infection is going to get very, very bad. Today, I shared my concerns with Eric and decided to write to family members, friends, and my shamanic colleagues about my concern, encouraging them all to prepare. If I'm wrong, so be it, and they can blow me off. It's just not worth taking a chance.

By early March, when the first officially recognized cases of Covid-19 had appeared on the West Coast of the United States, Eric and I were prepared for self-isolation. His boss agreed to allow him to do his I.T. work from home, and we used our extra time together to prepare the space for his blacksmith shop as guided by our *landvaettir*. It gave us a much needed sense of purpose in such a very uncertain time.

When the smithy structure was completed, it was Eric's desire to prepare the building for its service in a sacred way. The Duergar had generously assisted in making resources available for the building's construction, so the ceremony was planned to focus on deepening our connection with our kinsmen and honoring the heritage we carry. Prior to the ceremony, the Duergar had made clear that they would appreciate an offering of good Scotch and that oak was especially sacred to them. They also asked for a raspberry jelly-filled doughnut — mostly, I suspect, to see what hoops Eric would be willing to jump through.

We agreed that the building should be cleansed with Sacred Smoke and hallowed with Sacred Fire. So, I made a torch using a hazel branch, since hazel is a fire plant and often used within the Northern Traditions to mark out sacred spaces.

Tonight, we dedicated and hallowed Eric's blacksmith shop. I gathered the drinking horn I had made for him with the help of the Duergar, my fire kit, a mugwort recan stick, oak twigs, and kindling. We also took one of the small folding tables and a square of slate to protect the top from the heat of the fire. I wore Freyja's many strands of amber, my coat, and my hat.

We set up the little table with the slate on it and, then, the cauldron on that, while the drinking horn sat off to one side. I opened by singing the Hailing and, then, made a statement of intent that Eric elaborated. He stood facing me, and I used soot from his forge to draw paired Kenaz fire runes on his forehead, encouraging him to sing with me:

Fire, fire, heart of the forge
Burn in me, burn in me!

It took some time to get the fire started, but Eric worked on feeding oak twigs into the fire as I sang the song for Sacred Fire. I lit the recan stick and blew purifying mugwort smoke over the corners and walls as I walked anti-sunwise around the building. While Eric circumnavigated around the outside of the smithy with the lit torch, I sang to the Ancestors. Then, as he again circled the smithy, this time filling the drinking horn with fine Scotch, he poured out generous libations for the Duergar, and I sang their song.

They conveyed to me that they had assisted me in the creation of the drinking horn, having foreseen that it would one day be used to honor them in the hallowing of this smithy. It gives me great joy to see my beloved partner engaging in this craft.

I received a call from a client regarding a tract of land in the Blue Ridge near the little mountain town of Sparta. On a Saturday, we drove the winding roads for me to do an assessment on the property where she and her husband planned to build a home. The land came complete with a tiny old cemetery, and my client was especially interested in how to be good neighbors to her Dead Folks.

We parked near the little shady knoll where the cemetery stood and put on our masks. After introducing ourselves, I explained a bit about what I would be doing. Just because someone hires a shaman doesn't mean that they know much—if anything—about what said shaman will do. Fortunately, this woman was very open. A big part of my work was simply educating her about how to cultivate Right Relationship with her land.

After kindling Sacred Fire, I lit a tightly-bundled recan stick of rosemary and had Eric cleanse me with the smoke. Then, he took my shaman's coat out of its storage bag and held it so that I could slide my arms into the thick, soft sleeves. The fragrance of the leather enveloped me, and my awareness began to shift and open. Next, he settled my antler headpiece on my head and tied it snugly beneath my chin.

As soon as I was kitted out and began singing to call the Holy Powers and the Ancestors, a pair of kestrels soared over us, crying and playing. Immediately, I thought of the falcon feathered cloak Freyja wears and of Her ability to shape-shift. I staked the boundaries of the graveyard with four iron stakes Eric had forged, as there should always be some sort of demarcation between the realm of the Living and that of the Dead. I poured out water on the headstones and made offerings of coins and tobacco. Then, I taught my client simple ways to honor those Dead who had become her Dead by virtue of her purchase of the land. Afterwards, we walked over the property, and I shared my perceptions and suggestions for engaging more spiritually with her land.

Despite the pandemic, I had received apprenticeship inquiries from several potential students. Following divination, I declined two who were clearly troubled. Another young man had visited several times to talk with me about Animism and learn more about the beliefs of his Nordic ancestors. To honor his 35th birthday, he asked whether he could undertake a four day fast – something he had long planned for – on the sacred land of TwoTrees. After much discussion and positive divination, Eric and I gave permission. This experience was to lead to him becoming my first student-in-residence. My spirits encouraged me to offer him my mostly empty studio in exchange for his help with chores, and we entered into a ten-week-long arrangement that proved rewarding for both of us.

Later that year, another apprentice was able to come for a pandemic-safe visit, and I continued to meet the needs of clients as best I could during such difficult times. As the pandemic brought more and more deaths, I was ever more aware of a backlog of Dead Folks awaiting transition but unable to do so. Other spirit worker colleagues were experiencing the same awareness. At this time, much of my ceremonial energy was devoted to easing the crossing for the dead and dying.

Surrounded by a world filled with fear and grief, I felt the deep need to create, to affirm life.

All religions have their own particular icons and spiritual imagery. Among Norse, Germanic, and Slavic people of the pre-conversion era, it was common to raise carved votive images of their revered Gods. Often such godpoles, the term by which these are now known, served as a place of conversation with and offering to the represented deity. It seems likely that this practice was an outgrowth of the ancient practice of designating certain trees as Holy. With a renewed interest in pre-Christian spiritual practices, modern Heathens are considering ways to honor the Gods, and the carving and placing of godpoles is experiencing resurgence.

Our first godpoles were very simple, and Freyr's, being made of hickory, only lasted a couple of years. Although I'd done numerous smaller votive carvings, I had never undertaken something of size. Still, I began to feel compelled to attempt carving a substantial replacement pole for the Lord of Sacrifice out of eastern red cedar. While this fragrant, reddish wood is not related to Freyr in the lore, it has the advantage of being common here at TwoTrees and of resisting rot. Eric and I surveyed the hillside and found several trees of appropriate size. I dowsed each of them seeking the best candidate. A tall, straight tree about 35 years old and close to 12 inches in diameter at the base indicated it was willing to be harvested.

As we always do before cutting a tree here at TwoTrees, I asked the tree's permission, made offerings, and gave thanks for its role in the ecosystem. After binding off the base of the trunk with red thread, I asked the life force to depart the tree and flow outward to benefit the land. I laid my hands upon the trunk and felt the vital force slowly ebbing. When it had stilled, I stepped back and signaled Eric that the tree was ready to be felled. He started the chainsaw, and I began to drum, pushing any remaining energy into the earth. The tree swayed and fell gently onto a deep cushion of dead leaves and ferns. As I ever do, even when a tree is cut down out of necessity, I felt an ache and a sense of sadness.

Freyr is a God of love and sacrifice, the Grain Lord who willingly gives His life each year so His people will thrive, only to be resurrected as He springs forth from the warming earth. The first step of the carving process was to strip away the wonderfully useful fibrous bark, symbolic of Freyr's willingness to give of Himself for others. Among many Native American cultures, cedar bark was an important resource, being finely shredded for use as absorbent filler in infant cradleboards, providing fire tinder, or twined into strong cordage. The sapwood beneath is ivory in color and faintly piney in fragrance, revealing a loosely spiral growth pattern reminiscent of our DNA. Deeper in, the heartwood of cedar is deep rose and sweetly aromatic, often used in the construction of cedar chests and closets for the moth-proof storage of woolens.

As a fertility God, Freyr is often associated with phallic imagery, so I roughed out a somewhat helmet-shaped head that hinted at other symbolism. I sharpened a set of wood gouges and chisels, recaned my tools with sacred smoke, and blessed them before starting to carve. Working at a larger scale than my prior carvings brought its own set of challenges. The work proceeded slowly; I found I was able to carve for about an hour each morning and afternoon before my back knotted up.

Still, I persisted, often singing to Freyr as I freed Him from the wood. Carving is a process of starting from the outside and working toward the inside, revealing the intended object as more and more material is removed. The process, as always, brought back so many memories of watching my father carving, a craft he pursued throughout his life.

I had chosen an image of Freyr based on many traditional Viking Age depictions, with a long, straight nose, wide, staring eyes, and a neatly trimmed mustache and beard. Bit by bit, I chipped away, deepening the relief, shaping, and detailing. I also marked out and carved the rune *Inguz* — associated with Freyr's sacrifice and harvest — further down the pole.

The tale is told of how Freyr took advantage of the All-Father's High Seat to spy out across the worlds, and, while doing so, He saw the Jötun maiden Gerd and lost His heart. His attempts at wooing Her were repeatedly rebuffed until, at last, He gave up His fine sword, which had been enchanted and given to Him by His own mother, to prove the depth of His love. He gave it up knowing that He would never again have another with which to defend Himself. In its place, He took up an antler, another symbol of masculine potency.

While I was busy carving, Eric forged a u-shaped iron staple that we would use to fasten an antler to the pole. As I neared completion of the carving, I also cut two almond-shaped eyes from a sheet of bronze and mounted them. To give the image warmth and presence, I ground red ocher, that rusty iron-based mineral our ancestors associated with blood and life force, using the ruddy stain to tint the details of the carving. Finally, I cut out a groove to accept the antler and, with Eric's help, pinned it in place with the iron staple.

Our plan was to erect the pole at noon on the summer solstice, the moment of bright Sunna's greatest potency. We hallowed the hole dug to receive the pole with offerings of milk, honey, barley, and beer, afterward feasting on foods associated with the Golden One: crisply roasted pork with steamed grains, glossy red cherries, and, in the sweet spirit of mid-summer, a rich lemon sour cream pound cake.

Gift of the cedar, Freyr's godpole stands proudly overlooking the glade. A second godpole carved in the spring of

2021 honors my Lady Freyja, who now gazes down upon our sacred space with an impish grin. I have come to understand that my own dual nature reflects these Sacred Twins, and, increasingly, when I fill out forms that request my gender, I write "Shaman."

My sacred work goes on. I write, I create, I teach, and I heal.

My phone chimes, and I answer.

A hesitant female voice asks, "Do you ever work with children?" The woman tells me of her pre-teen daughter who is visited by the Dead and who senses things others do not. "She's so sensitive and anxious," the mom tells me, "and I don't know what to do. I asked her what she thought might help, and she said she wanted to talk to someone who experienced things like she does."

I remember my own younger self, my bewilderment and longing for guidance, and then I propose when and where we might meet. A shaman serves a community, even when they don't always know who is part of that community.

We meet in a room at 18 Springs, our faces masked, seated safely apart. The girl's dark, intelligent eyes sparkle over her mask, wide with recognition as I start by sharing a bit about my own childhood. "You're not the only one," I tell her. "I know it's tough, but there are things you can do that will make it easier to manage your Gifts."

As I explain, she nods, and somehow I know she's smiling.

People see me in my shaman's coat and antler headdress and ask what in the world I'm doing, because they don't understand. I'm doing spiritual archaeology. I'm hunkered down in the bitter dark, wind whipping around me, desperately trying to keep a tiny pile of embers alight until someone comes along with more fuel.

I do this for my Ancestors and for those to come, knowing that, without careful tending, the fire can go out. Sometimes someone comes along who brings fuel that catches quickly and burns brightly but is quickly consumed. Once that person has warmed at the fire and taken up a burning brand, they head back out into the darkness. Their torch may kindle others or go out; I'll never know.

My job is to keep the fire alight and share it. And, rarely, someone comes with good hardwood, makes camp, prepares to settle in, and, perhaps, just perhaps, will survive me to tend the fire for others.

The Calling

"Why a shaman?" you asked,
Puzzled by my curious life,
My coat of charms and horse-hide drum,
The signs of power inked upon my skin.

Because I heard the spirits of my Ancestors
Singing on the North Wind, and the
Silent wing beats of owls,
Hooves thundering upon the steppe
Carrying me eastward,
Into the vastness of the tundra.
There I sparkled against the dark,
Spun upward in a campfire's swirl,
And saw, upon the tender leaves of willows,
My reflection in bright beads of dew.

More than ever, you need me
And those like me,
Who remember when we danced
As sisters of earth and brothers of sky.
My work calls the shattered
Into wholeness and
My drum echoes the world's heartbeat,
A song to lift up all Beings.

Susannah Ravenswing   2021

GLOSSARY

Adak: A Mongolian votive structure to which prayer scarves are tied.

Aesir: A group of Norse Gods described in the lore as residing in Asgard, the world located at the top of the World Tree.

Alfar: Youthful-appearing Beings described in Norse lore and folk tales as dwelling in forests and near springs; the Elves. They can look like humans and sometimes intermarry with them. The dark elves are said to live above ground in Svartalfheim, whereas the bright elves live in Ljóssálfheim.

Allies: The Gods and spirits with whom one has established and cultivated reciprocal relationships, who lend assistance in shamanic workings.

Animism: The belief, common in many Indigenous cultures, that all things are enspirited and thus are Beings.

Asgard: In Norse cosmology, the world of the Aesir, located in the highest boughs of the World Tree, Yggdrasil.

Bagshagui: A Buryat Mongol word meaning "spirit taught."

Bindrune: A magical sigil created with specific intent through the overlaying of two or more runes.

Blót: A Heathen ceremony honoring the Gods through ritual offering or sacrifice.

Chakra: From the Sanskrit word *cakra,* one of a number of centers in the body where life force is believed to focus. Open, balanced chakras are associated with good health. The chakra system is not part of traditional shamanism, although many cultures have their own system of energy centers located in the human body.

Core Shamanism: The universal, near-universal, and common features of shamanism, together with journeys to other worlds, a distinguishing feature of shamanism. As originated, researched, and developed by Michael Harner, the principles of Core Shamanism are not bound to any specific cultural group or perspective.

Divination: The sacred art of providing insight and guidance accessed through various tools, such as the Runes, Tarot cards, stones, or bones, and a mildly altered state of consciousness.

Diviner: A practitioner of the sacred art of divination.

Dowsing: The art of locating targets such as underground water sources or gaining information through the use of specific tools such as Y- or L-rods or pendulums.

Duergar: The Dwarves, famed makers of sacred and magical tools in Norse tales and sagas who reside underground in the world of Svartalfheim.

Dysmorphia: A condition in which one's perceptions of their body differ from the reality of their body.

Entheogens: Those plants and fungi causing altered consciousness by virtue of their impact on the body's chemistry; held as sacred in some Indigenous cultures and by some spirit workers.

Eddas: The collections of stories and poems that constitute the primary early record of Norse and Icelandic mythology. They were primarily penned in the 13th century, the *Prose Edda* by the Icelandic Christian scholar and poet Snorri Sturluson.

Freyja: The Norse Goddess of love, sex, passion, beauty, magic, and war. She is of the Vanic tribe but was accepted as a peace hostage by the Aesir after the Aesir-Vanir War. Freyja is associated with gold, amber, honey, and cats. Her name, which means "Lady" in Old Norse, is also spelled Freja and Freyia. Freyja rules over her hall, Sessrúmnir, located in her heavenly field, Fólkvang, where she receives the first half of those who die in battle. The other half go to the God Odin's hall, Valhöll or Valhalla. Freyja is often confused with Frigga, Queen of Asgard.

Freyr: The Norse God of virility, prosperity, fair weather, good harvest, and sacred kingship. The Gods presented him with the world Ljossalfheim as a teething present. He is a member of the Vanic tribe, the twin brother of Freyja and, like her, accepted as a peace hostage following the Aesir-Vanir War. Freyr or Frey, whose name means "Lord," is associated with boars, horses, nuts, grain, and self-sacrifice.

Frith: An Old Norse term meaning good-will.

Galdr, Galdred: To intone the name or a rune or runes in such a way as to engage its spirit.

Geomancy: The art of optimizing the energetic well-being of a parcel of land, akin to Chinese Feng Shui.

God-Owned: A term referencing an individual whose life is given over to the service of a particular deity and whose mental health and physical wellness are dependent upon service to that deity.

Gothi, Godhi: A Heathen priest.

Gythja: A female Heathen priest.

Harrow: A Heathen altar or place of offering, often a large stone or tree.

Heathen: One who practices the pre-Christian religion of the ancient Germanic people, or a modern reconstruction thereof, and worships the Germanic and Norse Gods. The term is also used pejoratively by some to mean someone who is ignorant and non-Christian.

Hel (also: Hela): The Norse Goddess of Death who rules over Helheim. She has nothing to do with the Christian concept of hell.

Helheim: In Norse cosmology, the world of the Dead, lowest on the World Tree in many interpretations.

Holy Powers: The Gods, Ancestors, and spirits.

Hörgr: A Heathen altar or place of offering, of piled or stacked stones.

Intersex: Individuals born with any of several variations in sex characteristics including chromosomes, gonads, sex hormones, or genitals.

Jötun, Jötnar: The Norse Giants or Elemental Beings.

Jötunheim: In Norse cosmology, the world of the Jötnar.

Journey, Journeying: To enter non-ordinary consciousness and travel to other worlds.

Khernips: A consecrated liquid used in spiritual cleansing, from the Hellenic Tradition.

Khatag: Mongolian prayer scarves, often made of silk and dyed a deep sky blue.

Landvaettir: The Norse term for the spirit of a given place.

LGBTIQ: An acronym meaning Lesbian, Gay, Bisexual, Transgender, Intersex, or Queer.

Ljóssálfheim: In Norse cosmology, the world of the Light Elves, ruled by Freyr.

Magic: The art of using will and intention to alter reality.

Mani: The Moon in Norse cosmology, seen as masculine.

Midgard: In Norse cosmology, the world of humankind.

Muspelheim: In Norse cosmology, the primal world of Fire, ruled by Surtr.

Neopaganism: A modern religious movement that seeks to incorporate beliefs or ritual practices from traditions outside the main world religions, especially those of pre-Christian Europe and North America.

Neoshamanism: A New Age variant of Core Shamanism not grounded in any particular culture or religion, often emphasizing improvisation, ceremonial elements drawn from a variety of cultures, and the use of psychedelic drugs.

Niflheim: In Norse cosmology, the primal world of Ice.

Nine Worlds: The worlds supported by the World Tree Yggdrasil in Norse cosmology: Asgard, Ljóssálfheim, Vanaheim, Jötunheim, Midgard, Svartalfheim, Muspelheim, Niflheim, and Helheim.

Noaidi: A Sámi shaman.

Ochre: A mineral containing a large amount of iron, ranging from yellow to deep reddish-brown, frequently ground and used as a pigment.

Odin ("OHDTH-in," called Wotan or Woden in Germanic lore): A Norse God of war, magic, and shape-shifting, whose name means "Frenzy." Lusty God of ecstasy, storm, hunting, poetry, berserk fury, and incantations. A member of the Aesir and husband of Frigga.

Ordeal: (A) A difficult and often painful experience undergone as part of shamanic training and initiation. (B) An especially challenging experience.

Paganism: Any of many religions primarily focused on nature. The term is often applied pejoratively to non-Christians.

Portal: A doorway between one time, place, or reality and another.

Recan, Recaning: To cleanse with sacred smoke, akin to the Native American practice of smudging.

Runebom: A Sámi word for large shaman's drums often bearing symbols of significant deities, spirits, or worlds on the drumhead.

Runes: A pictographic alphabet held by some to be of divine origin, and by archeolinguists to be derived from the Roman alphabet. In its later 24- and 36-character forms, referred to as Futhorcs or Futharcs, the Runes are often used in divination.

Sacred Smith: A craftsperson working in either precious metals or iron possessing the ability to imbue their work with magical and spiritual energies.

Sámi: The descendants of Finno-Ugric nomadic peoples who have inhabited northern Scandinavia and northwestern Russia for thousands of years.

Sastun: A Mayan word for a small, clear quartz pebble used as a seeing stone.

Seidhkona: A Norse term for a female capable of entering a trance state and acting as a medium or oracle.

Seidr, Seidhr: The Norse word for magical and shamanic

practices including spell-work, sex magic, and spae or vision-ary mediumship.

Sessrúmnir: Freyja's hall, located in a field called Fólkvang in the world of Asgard.

Shagai: A Mongolian divination technique utilizing four sheep ankle bones.

Shaman: An initiated spiritual practitioner who makes use of alliances with the Holy Powers of their culture or tradition and achieves altered states of consciousness, allowing them to journey to non-ordinary reality, thus serving their community as a counselor and healer.

Shamanic Initiation: A ritual, often including some form of ordeal, in which the initiate must prove their ability to engage with the Holy Powers and during which they receive a trans-mission of lineage, energy, and elevated consciousness. Such an event may be public or secret and marks the transition from apprentice to Shaman.

Shamanic Practitioner: An uninitiated individual who works with shamanic techniques.

Sigil: A graphic symbol used in the act of magic.

Skald: A Norse term referencing someone with the bardic gift, capable of creating songs of power.

Spaekona: A Norse term for a woman who serves as a Seer and Oracle. Some practitioners use the term Seidhkona.

SPG: Shared Personal Gnosis, the insights or revelations inde-pendently experienced by multiple individuals; peer-corrobo-rated information.

Soul Map: A divination technique exploring the strengths, weaknesses, blocks, and other aspects of the human soul, as understood and used as a healing tool by some practitioners of the Northern Tradition.

Standing Stones of Callanish: A large megalithic stone circle, constructed between 4900 and 4600 B.C.E. on the island of Lewis off the northwest coast of Scotland.

Sumbel (also: Symbel): A formal drinking ritual composed of toasting, hails, oath-taking, the recitation of poetry or song, and other forms of verbal expression, based in accounts from written lore and practiced by modern Heathens.

Sunna: In Norse cosmology, the Sun, seen as feminine.

Svartalfheim: In Norse cosmology, the world inhabited above ground by the Svartalfar or Dark Elves and below ground by the Duergar or Dwarves.

Synesthesia: A neurological condition in which the senses are cross-wired, with numbers, colors, and musical pitches often interrelated.

Taiga: The boreal forest lies between the tundra to the north and temperate forests to the south. The cold, subarctic region is characterized by coniferous forests consisting mostly of pines, spruces, and larches.

Toli: A round metal disc, either plain or decorated, the function of which is to act as a mirror shield. Common in Mongolian and Siberian shamanism, toli may be worn over the shaman's chest or sewn to their coat.

Trance: An alteration in one's state of consciousness achieved intentionally or unintentionally.

UPG: Unverified Personal Gnosis, the insights or revelations experienced by an individual and held as true by them

Utiseta: An Old Norse term meaning "Out-sitting" or "Going under the cloak." A traditional form of trance journey in which the practitioner, wrapped in a cloak or blanket, uses a particular rhythmic breathing to enter an altered state. Often done on a burial mound or other sacred site.

Vaet: A Norse term for a spirit.

Vaettir: A Norse term referencing the spirits of land and place.

Vaettir Kista: Old Norse for "spirit chest": a box or small trunk for storing small shamanic tools.

Vanadis: Lady of Vanaheim, an honorific for Freyja.

Vanaheim: In Norse cosmology, the world of the Vanir, a tribe of Gods governing agriculture and herding.

Vanir: A group of Norse Gods described in the lore as residing in either Vanaheim or as peace hostages in Asgard.

Varthlokkur: An Old Norse term referring to a spell-song or chant that offers protection for a Spaekona and aids in triggering her trance.

Ve: A Norse term for a sacred or hallowed place, often where offerings are made.

VPG: Verified Personal Gnosis, the insights or revelations experienced independently by several individuals, Peer Corroborated Knowledge.

Völva: A Norse wise woman, seer, healer, or witch highly respected in pre-Christian times. (Note: the English word "heal" reaches back through German and Icelandic to words for "holy" and "whole.") Males who held an analogous role were known as **vitkar** (singular **vikti**).

Ward: A form of magical protection.

Wicca: A form of modern Paganism.

Wight: An Anglo-Saxon term for a spirit; a vaet.

Wight Cake: A small loaf, traditionally of flour, butter, honey, and milk, created as a votive offering to the land spirits.

Yggdrasil: The Norse World Tree or axis mundi, upon which are arranged the Nine Worlds of the Norse cosmology.

RELATED READINGS

Northern Traditions

Neolithic Shamanism: Spirit Work in the Norse Tradition,
Raven Kaldera and Galina Krasskova. Destiny Books, 2012.

An introductory text appropriate for individuals interested in the shamanic practices of Scandinavia and northern Eurasia.

A Modern Guide to Heathenry: Lore, Celebrations and
Traditions of the Northern Traditions,
Galina Krasskova. Weiser Books, 2019.

An excellent introduction to modern Heathenism.

The Viking Way: Magic and Mind in Late Iron Age
Scandinavia,
Neil Price. Oxbow Books, 2013 and 2019.

An in-depth and scholarly text exploring prior assumptions about Norse magical practices and current archaeological perspectives.

Sky Shamans of Mongolia: Meetings with Remarkable Healers,
Kevin Turner. Atlantic Books, 2016.

An account of Turner's encounters with Mongolian shamans and healers.

Fire Jewel: A Devotional for Freyja,
Gefion Vanirdottir. Asphodel Press, 2013.

A collection of essays, prayers, rituals and excerpts from traditional lore honoring the Goddess Freyja.

The Duergarbok: The Dwarves of the Northern Tradition,
Susannah Ravenswing. Asphodel Press, 2019.

Continue your journey with Susannah Ravenswing while she shares about her research and relationship with the Duergar.

Creation's Heartbeat: Following the Reindeer Spirit,
Linda Schierse Leonard. Bantam Books, 1995.

A deep and thoughtful exploration of the history and significance of Reindeer as an embodiment of the Divine Feminine.

Other Spiritual Resources

Ancestral Medicine: Rituals for Personal and Family Healing,
Daniel Foor. Bear and Company Books, 2017.

An excellent introduction for those interested in engaging with their Ancestors.

Woman in the Shaman's Body: Reclaiming the Feminine in Religion and Medicine,
Barbara Tedlock. Bantam Dell, 2005.

A thoughtful and poignant exploration of the rich history of women as healers and conduits of the holy.

Spiritual Protection: A Safety Manual for Energy Workers, Healers and Psychics,
Sophie Richter. New Page Books, 2010.

Fundamental theory and practices to help individuals to ground, center and shield, as well as ways of protecting against negative energies.

The Home Place: Memoirs of a Colored Man's Affair with Nature,
J. Drew Lanham. Milkweed Editions, 2017.

The author, an ornithologist and professor of wildlife ecology, shares his deeply moving relationship with nature through the lens of his childhood and culture.

Braiding Sweetgrass: Indigenous Wisdom, Scientific Knowledge and the Teachings of Plants.
Robin Wall Kimmerer. Milkweed Editions, 2013.

An exquisitely written exploration of animism and sacred reciprocity from a Native American perspective.

Sex and Gender Resources

The Spectrum of Sex: The Science of Male, Female,
and Intersex,
Hida Viloria and Maria Nieto. Jessica Kingsley Publishers, 2020.

An accessible, entertaining, and comprehensive introduction to the science of sex development and intersex variations.

How to Understand Your Gender: A Practical Guide for Ex-
ploring Who You Are,
Alex Iantaffi and Meg-John Barker. Jessica Kingsley Publishers, 2017.

An introductory workbook for thinking about how sex and gender, bodies, culture, and identity all fit together in your own life as well as in the world around us.

Born Both: An Intersex Life,
Hida Viloria. Hachette Books, 2017.

This autobiography by a leading intersex advocate emphasizes self-acceptance and love.

Traversing Gender: Understanding Transgender Realities,
Lee Harrington. Mystic Productions Press, 2016.

An accessible text offering information, resources and support for transgender people and their families, written by a well-known activist and sex-positive educator.

Transgender Warriors: Making History from Joan of Arc to
Dennis Rodman, Leslie Feinberg. Beacon Press, 1996.

This classic book by a transgender author traces gender diversity through history, helping us begin to ground our current lives in a rich history of gender transcendent ancestors.

My Gender Workbook: How to Become a Real Man, a Real Woman, the Real You, or Something Else Entirely and My New Gender Workbook: A Step-by-Step Guide to Achieving World Peace Through Gender Anarchy and Sex Positivity, *Kate Bornstein.* Routledge, 1998 and 2013.

This classic text provides an irreverent but dynamic exploration of sex, gender, and much, much more.

Queer Embodiment: Monstrosity, Medical Violence, and Intersex Experience, *Hilary Malatino.* University of Nebraska, 2019.

This academic treatment is an early intervention in the field of critical intersex studies. Offered by an intersex scholar, this work draws together threads from from medical ethics and humanities, gender studies, queer studies, and disability studies.

Neuro-Divergent Resources

NeuroTribes: The Legacy of Autism and the Future of Neurodiversity, *Steve Silberman.* Penguin/Random House, 2016.

Looks at neurological differences such as autism, dyslexia, and ADHD, not as errors of nature or products of the toxic modern world, but as natural variations.

Related Readings

The Power of Neurodiversity: Unleashing the Advantages of Your Differently Wired Brain,
Thomas Armstrong. Hachette Books, 2011.

Explores the evolutionary advantages, special skills, and other positive dimensions of conditions such as ADHD, dyslexia, and autism.

Uniquely Human: A Different Way of Seeing Autism,
Barry M. Prizant. Simon & Schuster, 2016.

Directed toward non-autistic communities, this book helps us all to understand autism as a normal part of human experience. Rather than "correcting" autistic people, Prizant helps us understand alternate ways of coping, communicating, and surviving.

We're Not Broken: Changing the Autism Conversation,
Eric Garcia. Mariner Books, 2021.

Combines memoir, history, interviews, advice, scientific research in order to help us change course from the mistreatment of autistic people.

ONLINE RESOURCES

Spiritual Resources

http://www.susannahravenswing.com

Susannah's website describes her shamanic practice and services offered and also includes her blog, "Tales from the World Tree."

https://www.facebook.com/SusannahRavenswingShaman

Susannah's shamanism Facebook page.

https://www.northernpaganism.org

An extensive resource website for individuals interested in Norse Paganism which includes general information, stories about the Gods, Their attributes, and prayers and virtual shrines honoring Them.

http://www.northernshamanism.org

Raven Kaldera's website, with information about his work and books.

http://ntsguild.org

Website for the Northern Tradition Shamanism Guild, providing information on training and guild-approved providers.

http://www.sacredhoop.org

A leading international magazine about shamanism, established in 1993.

https://www.facebook.com/groups/3WorldsShamanism

A social media group devoted to authentic shamanism and moderated by Nicholas Breeze Wood, the publisher of Sacred Hoop magazine.

https://shamanism.org/

Website for the Foundation for Shamanic Studies, founded by Michel Harner.

https://pluralism.org/

Harvard's Pluralism Project may be a good place to explore a variety of religious and spiritual perspectives.

Sex and Gender Resources

https://www.youtube.com/watch?v=czbQRjdGvYQ

The Intersexion documentary is a 2012 documentary (available on YouTube, 50 minute run time) which weaves together interviews of and reflections by intersex activists from around the world.

https://interactadvocates.org

A leading organization providing information, advocacy and resources supporting intersex persons and their friends, families and allies, including education to the medical profession.

https://isna.org

While the Intersex Society of North America shut down years ago, the website remains an important historic resource.

http://www.traversinggender.com

A growing collection of resources for transgender and gender diverse people, friends, family, allies, and medical providers.

https://pflag.org

PFLAG originally stood for "Parents and Friends of Lesbians and Gays," but provides a good starting place for local networking about LGBT resources in particular.

https://www.glaad.org/resourcelist

There are many organizations working on different areas of LGBT concern. This is just one list focusing on such resources.

Neuro-Divergent Resources

https://www.neurodiversity-celebration-week.com/

Neurodiversity Celebration Week works to educate and advocate for neuro-diversity in the classroom.

https://neurogifted.com/

Promoting neurodiversity by eliminating stigma, providing resources, celebrating strengths, and opening the doors of opportunity for neurodivergents.

https://community.autastic.com/

Online community by and for autistic people, including those exploring diagnosis as adults.

https://uniquelyhuman.com/

Podcast from the author of *Uniquely Human*.

https://instagram.com/myautisticsoul

A blog by an individual focused on advocacy for queer and autistic folks and those struggling with mental health issues.

https://drkimberlydouglass.com

Dr. Douglass is autistic herself and speaks on intersectionality within the autistic community.

https://www.facebook.com/groups/thatausomebookclub/

"That Au-some Book Club" Facebook group is a book club with lists of books curated by autistic people.

https://notanautismmom.com

Not An Autism Mom is a website with excellent resources for parents, children and educators.

Acknowledgements

This book could not have been written without the support and encouragement of many Beings, and I fear I will not remember everyone who deserves acknowledgement. Gratitude is fundamental to *Gebo*, Sacred Exchange, and I am truly and deeply grateful.

Hail to the Holy Powers, the Numinous and Infinite Mysteries that are ever willing to reveal Themselves when we are observant. I honor my Lady, Freyja, who saved my life and whom I gladly serve.

Hail to my Ancestors, without whom I would not exist. In the DNA that was your legacy, I received numerous gifts for which I am profoundly grateful, and I am blessed by your guidance every day.

Hail to the *Vaettir*, the spirits of Nature, of weather, of place, and of Being. I am grateful for your instruction and willingness to aid me in my work.

I honor the Wise Ones and practitioners before me, the herbalists and healers, the medicine folk, the witches, the oracles and diviners, the polytheists who honor many Gods, the shamans of rainforest and tundra persecuted and destroyed by Church and State, and the bards and storytellers who passed on their legacy of old lore and sacred tales.

I honor those willing to be open to the possibility that the generally held and promoted concept of reality is rigid, polarizing, disempowering, and plain old unimaginative.

Acknowledgments

I honor those who, by virtue of their life choices, choose to be responsible for their impact on the environment, recognizing that we will survive or go extinct together.

I honor my Kinfolk of the Liminal, those whose sense of gender is transcendent and who understand the wonder, power, and healing to be found on The Road Less Traveled.

I honor the Indigenous people who once called the Carolina Piedmont home, the Keyauwee, Catawba, Sissapahaw, and the Saura People, on whose land I now reside.

I honor the Beings of TwoTrees, with whom I share my daily life. You are friends, teachers, playmates, and daily fill my life with wonder, joy, and beauty.

I honor my late parents, Cedric and Emily Squires, who found me puzzling and challenging and loved me as best they could. I miss you both on this side of the veil and can show you a great shortcut to Scotland if you're interested.

I honor my teachers, especially my aunt Ruamie Squires and my grandmother Ethel Carroll Squires, who unlocked the worlds of art, literature, and history for me, as well as Ken Bradstock, who showed me what a teacher should be. He helped me to believe in myself and my Calling.

I bless my Northern Tradition Elders, Raven Kaldera and Galina Krasskova, whose scholarship and gnosis offered me a map through dark times. I also bless my colleagues in this tradition: don't let the flame go out!

I bless my Wise Women Elders: Marea Streat, Sue Strauss, and Kirtan Koan, who encouraged my creative efforts, listened to my struggles, and affirmed my spiritual and artistic explorations. My life has been so much richer thanks to all of you.

I bless those who kept saying, "Hey, you really ought to write a book!" — Kirtan, Sidney, Ken, Peggy, and Alec, among so many others. Blessings, too, to Liam, who has done so much to make this dream a reality and who continues to inspire me with his courage.

I bless the beta readers, who took on my first draft and offered great suggestions, who red-penciled, wrangled commas, and let me know when I was being unclear or redundant. Kate, Nancy, Deborah, Julie, Cindi, and especially Peggy — thank you all. I am deeply grateful to Diana Coe, whose skill and artistry gave this book vision and soul.

I bless those who harmed me, for you were the forge, hammer, and anvil that shaped and hardened my steel.

I bless the therapists and healers with whom I've worked over the years, who helped me better understand this strange business of being human and encouraged me to thrive in my most curious, self-made life.

I bless my Heart-Sister Kristy Bartley, whose love and support have sustained me, and who, by virtue of her courage, compassion, and willingness to speak truth to power, inspires me daily to make a difference in this world.

I am filled with deep love and gratitude for my sons Blake and Christopher, who somehow survived having a strange mom. You teach me every day what it means to be "good people," and you brought me amazing daughters in the strong women you married. You and your families are my heart's legacy to this beautiful world.

My beloved Eric — You are my refuge. I struggle to find the words to say what your enduring love and support have meant to me every single day. Being the spouse of a shaman is almost as hard as actually being a shaman. Nevertheless, you have tirelessly schlepped drums and offerings over hill and dale, driven me to ceremonies when it wasn't safe for me to drive myself, held me when I shook with exhaustion afterwards, and done so many, many things to make it possible for me to serve the Holy Powers we both revere. Early in our friendship, you invoked "more silliness" at a ritual, and see where it got you!

Susannah Ravenswing
May 1, 2021

About the Author

Susannah Ravenswing is an author, artist, musician, and healer whose work is rooted in Nature and the sacred traditions of pre-Christian Northern Europe and Eurasia. Born intersex and neurodivergent, she transcended a remarkable series of traumas and ordeals to create a profoundly meaningful life through the interweaving of her creative and intuitive gifts.

During a long career as a gold and silversmith, she specialized in sacred and collegiate regalia, creating the chalice used in the reconsecration of Britain's famed Stonehenge and achieving coveted Exhibitor Emerita status in the nationally recognized Piedmont Craftsman Guild.

Years spent studying how her Celtic, Norse, and Germanic ancestors engaged with the natural world prepared her for the greatest test of all, a near-death experience in which she was called by the Norse Goddess Freyja to become an apprentice in the Northern shamanic traditions.

As a specialist shaman, healer, and ritualist, Susannah focuses on eco-animism, rewilding, and sacred reciprocity with the natural world and the spirits present in everything surrounding us. In addition to caring for clients, training her apprentices, and teaching workshops, she serves as an Elder and ally to the Northern Shamanism Guild.

Susannah resides with her husband Eric, a blacksmith, and their cats, on sacred land in the rugged Saura Hills of northwestern North Carolina. In addition to *Singing to the North*

Wind: The Calling to an Extraordinary Life, she is also the author of *The Duergerbok: The Dwarves of the Northern Tradition*.

You can reach her through her website:
http://www.susannahravenswing.com/

More Praise for
Susannah Ravenswing's Work...

"Absolutely the real deal! She has been on her journey for the thirty years or more I have known her. A warm wise woman in the ancient tradition of shamans."

~ David G.

"If you are fortunate, you will meet an 'old soul,' someone with wisdom beyond their years. If you are amazingly lucky, you'll discover that person is able to see the world with 'new eyes,' that is, able to look beyond the obvious, rethinking what they 'know.' And if you are favored beyond that, you'd meet Susannah, who sees the world that was and the world that can be, while being grounded in the world that is.

"My life has been enriched by her willingness to both embrace the world and to challenge me to make my life better. She is able to balance trusting, compassion, and growth with the necessary skills of defense, boundary setting, and leaving behind. She teaches both by example and through thoughtful advice and structured workshops. I can think of no better guide to help me live a fully actualized life."

~ Kate J.

"Susannah is authenticity itself. She is deeply spiritual and wholly connected to Things Unseen. She is well-steeped in Northern Tradition lore and actively resonates with it. She is a mover and a shaker (i.e., a reading or healing work with her and your energy will not be in the same places and patterns it was before she entered your life! An exceedingly talented Maker as well—her jewelry is just stunning. I wholeheartedly recommend her to the questing seeker!"

~ Chris C.

"Susannah immediately puts you at ease, offering a safe space for exploring goals and recognizing opportunities for growth and change, inviting you into a powerful relationship of stwardship with yourself. Highly recommend!"

~ Ali R.

"Having never visited a shaman, I had no clue what to expect. Susannah knew just what questions to ask and amazed me by the things she intuitively knew about me. Our initial meeting resulted in her creating a special personal ceremony that was deeply healing for me, and our work together h as helped me move forward in my life."

~ Michael K.

"Susannah, I can only say thank you, to you and your Guides, for this Soul Map reading. There is a lot in it that surprised me, but I also have a sense of recognition—like I've been waiting for someone to tell me these truths in such a clear way. There is depth, and so many facets to this divination—I know I will return to it frequently, to guide me on my way. I would recommend your work to anyone who is looking for objective, yet deeply spiritual, guidance. What a gift!"

~ Jonathan E.

"I've been going through a difficult period, and found myself facing some tough choices. A friend recommended that I have a Soul Map reading done by Susannah, and it was worth every penny. She helped me recognize obstacles I'd overlooked and offered insights that have helped me move forward more confidently."

~ Marshall N.

"Getting a Soul Map interpretation from Susannah was a great decision for me. She was thorough both in the conversation and the explanation of what she was seeing. For me, I think it was spot on and extremely helpful in upcoming choices that I needed to make. The follow-up information to help solidify the reading was detailed and a nice touch."

~ Sam T.

"My work with Susannah was deep and effective with lasting results. Transformative ripples are still unfolding from the intergenerational healing work we did together to heal alcoholism in my family lineage. I continue to experience profound positive changes that extend out to my relatives and beyond. Susannah provides presence and clarity in her shamanic work. She holds sacred space in a safe and powerful way."

~ Evangeline H.

"Following my separation from my very toxic partner, I kept feeling exhausted and experienced troubling nightmares. Susannah encouraged me to see a therapist, but she also did a ceremony that severed the energetic connection between me and my ex. I can't say how much better I feel now."

~ Maxxi C.

"I wasn't sure what to expect from my Soul Map reading, but Susannah immediately put me at ease. I was amazed by her insights and the detailed write-up she provided afterward has allowed me to make the maximum use of this valuable guidance. "

~ Rachel M.

"I asked Susannah to use the Runes to look at the prospects around my new practice, and she picked up on several concerns I'd overlooked. I left her office much more confident that I was taking the right steps."

~ Amy H.

"I am in the process of restoring a long underused piece of property and consulted with Susannah to work on the geomancy of the land in order to ensure that the work we are proposing to do is in accordance with what is best for the land and for its healing. With her deep understanding and connection with the land we are slowly rehabilitating and bringing back to life not only a neglected piece of property but also healing very old rifts and deep seated wounds that were not only destructive for the land but for those that occupied that land. It has been an extraordinary process and I am so grateful to have found Susannah and worked with her."

~ Peggy O.

"A friend suggested I contact Susannah to address the yucky energy in the house I bought. She was able to sense the sources of what I found troublesome and effectively removed the funk. My house feels great now!"

~ Lyn R.

"I was renovating an old farmhouse and the workmen kept complaining about someone misplacing or stealing their tools. There was also an area in the back of the house that none of them wanted to work in. Susannah's cleansing ceremony has made a huge difference."

~ Linda T.

"Lots of Tarot readers are vague, but I was amazed at how specific Susannah's divination was. The information wasn't exactly what I hoped for, but it was spot on, and the situation unfolded exactly as she'd foreseen."

~ Connie J.

"My husband and I purchased a tract of land in hopes of building a home there, only to discover it had been used as a dumping ground. Under Susannah's guidance, my relationship with my land has deepened and we have restored our property to balance and health."

~ Karen P.

"Susannah Ravenswing was pivotal in the shaping of the public Triad Pagan community 20+ years ago, mentoring the priesthood/leaders of many different groups/covens/groves, including ours. Her thirst for knowledge, dedication to the Path, and genuine heart are a gift to all those who are blessed to work with and know her!"

~ Clann C.

www.ingramcontent.com/pod-product-compliance
Lightning Source LLC
Chambersburg PA
CBHW011234120626
46549CB00009B/3267